Don't Never

A Physicist's Approach to Life

*For our friend Veronica
from the Author
Frederick M. Phelps III*

Copyright © 2015 Fritz Phelps
All rights reserved.
ISBN: 978-1516845477
ISBN-13: 1516845471

~~Dedication~~

This book has no dedication.

Don't Never, 4

Contents

- Preface 10
- Part I. Childhood Family Stories (1933-1939) 13
  - 1. Uncle Maurice and Aunt Peg 13
  - 2. Curtis, Michigan 15
    - a. The Cardboard Clothes 15
    - b. The Fire 16
    - c. The Model T 16
    - d. The Forest Fire 17
- Part II. School Days (1938-1951) 18
  - 3. Kindergarten Assignment – Draw a Picture of a Ship 18
  - 4. Third Grade Math – Multiplication 19
  - 5. Fourth Grade Math – Long Division 19
  - 6. Eighth Grade Math – Mrs. McGregor and Baseball 20
  - 7. Freshman Year in High School – The Ultimate Carpenter 22
  - 8. War in Mr. Sartwell's Class 24
  - 9. High School Algebra and Haydn's Creation 25
  - 10. High School Chemistry – Why I'm a Physicist and Not a Chemist 28
  - 11. High School Physics (1951) 30
- Part III. Carleton College (1951-1955) 32
  - 12. Why Carleton College? 32
  - 13. First Year at Carleton 33
  - 14. Dean Jarcho 35

- 15. PARTY AND PRESSURE POLITICS ... 36
- 16. THE MOUSE IN BURTON HALL ... 38

PART IV. SUMMER IN LOS ALAMOS (1955) ... 40
- 17. BEFORE THERE WERE CALCULATORS ... 40
- 18. THE 18 KILOGRAM WATERMELON ... 41
- 19. SPAGHETTI ... 42

PART V. GRADUATE SCHOOL, TAKE ONE (1955-1956) ... 44
- 20. SINKING INDEPENDENTLY WITH KASIMIR FAJANS ... 44
- 21. THERMODYNAMICS ... 46

PART VI. THE ARMY YEARS (1956-1958) ... 47
- 22. DON'T NEVER ... 47
- 23. INTO THE ARMY ... 47
- 24. THE PROFESSOR ... 49
- 25. WHEN TO VOLUNTEER ... 50
- 26. THE BAYONET COURSE ... 51
- 27. THE TOP SECRET ARMY CHEMICAL CENTER ... 53
- 28. CHRISTMAS ... 55
- 29. ENIWETOK ATOLL ... 57
- 30. A SHOWER OF ROCKS ... 58
- 31. COMPANY B DRIVES CAPTAIN TO THE KOREAN WAR .. 59
- 32. ORDERING PLUTONIUM ... 61
- 33. "HOW TO TELL TIME," BY SERGEANT ROCK ... 62
- 34. PHELPS JOINS THE TRAINING TEAM ... 64
- 35. THE RIFLE RANGE OR "LEARNING HOW TO SHOOT" 67
- 36. ONE WAY TO GET DISCHARGED FROM THE ARMY ... 70

PART VII. BACK TO GRADUATE SCHOOL (1958-1964) ... 74
- 37. CLOSED DOORS AND ON TO KALAMAZOO COLLEGE ... 74

- 38. TEACHING AT KALAMAZOO 76
- 39. PLANNING FOR A PH.D. 77
- 40. FINDING A MATHEMATICIAN FOR KALAMAZOO: JEAN CALLOWAY 78
- 41. THE MOVE TO EDMONTON (1960) 79
- 42. THE NORTHERN LIGHTS 81
- 43. PROFESSOR NEWBOUND 82
- 44. CANDIDACY EXAM 83
- 45. LEARNING TO WRITE COMPUTER PROGRAMS 85
- 46. PROFESSOR L. E. H. TRAINER (1962) 88
- 47. ENDOWED SCHOLARSHIPS 91

PART VIII. FAMILY STORIES (1960-PRESENT) 98

- 48. TRAINS, SUGAR WATER, AND OTHER THINGS 98
- 49. FRED IV'S MATHEMATICAL BIOLOGY – THE SEX OF CROCODILIANS 100
- 50. FRED IV'S MATHEMATICAL BIOLOGY – VISCERAL LEISHMANIASIS 100
- 51. FRED'S EARLY SPEECH 103
  - A. NORTH SASKATCHEWAN RIVER 103
  - B. NEW PESSER-BOUND 103
  - C. A VISIT TO WALLA WALLA 104
  - D. UNIVERSITY OF ALBERTA FOOTBALL 104
- 52. STORIES OF DOROTHY 105
  - A. FAVORITE BIRD 105
  - B. SKINNEY STREET 105
  - C. YOU NEED MORE PRACTICE! 106
- 53. RICHARD 107
- 54. SCOUTMASTER OF TROOP 628 108

55. A VERY SMART BLOND NAMED GINGER 110
56. THE AMANA COLONIES, IOWA 112
57. THE BAT 113
58. TAHQUAMENON FALLS AND THE GREAT LAKES SHIPWRECK MUSEUM 114
59. DOROTHY MEETS HER HUSBAND 116

PART IX. PROFESSOR AT CENTRAL MICHIGAN UNIVERSITY (1970-2012) 118

60. THE TRUE/FALSE EXAM 118
61. MY ANTI-RHODES SCHOLAR 119
62. MR. GORMLEY 120
63. THE EMINENT INDIVIDUAL 121
64. MUDDY PAW PRINTS IN PRE-MED PHYSICS 123
65. PROFESSOR BROMLEY AND THE CHRISTIAN FACULTY LUNCH 126
66. SARAH 128
67. TENSORS AND ELLEN 131
68. A WORD ON DIPLOMACY 133
69. TIFFANY AND BROTHER STONEKING 133
70. BRIAN 136
71. LAURA 138
72. AMY 140
73. ANN 141
74. MARIE 144
75. ERICA, PART 1 149
76. ERICA, PART 2 151

PART X. GINGER'S PHYSICS EXAM 154

77. PHYSICS PROBLEMS #1 ZOOMING 154

- 78. Physics Problems # 2-6 155
- 79. Problem # 7 Doppler's Effect 156
- 80. Problems # 8-12 de Broglie's Hypothesis 157
- 81. Problem #13 Ginger on Vector Addition 158
- 82. Problem #14 Gingerball 159

Final Word to the Reader 162

Preface

This is a collection of stories by my father, Frederick M. Phelps III, also known as "Fritz", who, among other things, was an Associate Professor of Physics at Central Michigan University for 42 years until he retired at age 79 in 2012.

My father has always been a storyteller. Once upon a time, more than forty years ago, he was telling me about his time in the army. He told me that one day he wanted to write a book about his experiences and that he would call it ***Don't Never***. That day has finally come, mostly because I reminded him of his ancient proclamation, and pushed him over the finish line with the help of my son, Kaile.

My purpose in pushing this project is to have a non-evolving permanent record of my father's stories. Despite the fact that most of us[1] would be happy if we sold millions of copies, our goals are essentially personal. Besides for relatives and others whose lives he has significantly impacted, this book probably holds minimal interest, despite a few historically significant gems: how Professor Fajan's escaped from Hitler's Germany, testing H-Bombs on Eniwetok Atoll and using IBM punch cards to program (without "debugging") the first computer at the University of Alberta.

Things of importance to my father shine through: his blond girlfriend Ginger,[2] Endowed Scholarships, and, most of all, his passion for "helping his students," as a way of paying back the kindness shown to him by his Ph.D. thesis advisor and Personal Hero, Professor Newbound.

---

[1] Some would say, the less publicity, the less embarrassment.
[2] She was 3/4^{ths} cocker spaniel.

This book would have been somewhat better if it had been written fifteen years ago, but Dad loved teaching[3] so much that he continued all the way until health issues forced him to retire at the age of 79. A proper editor would have done a more thorough job of gathering[4] and filtering the material, but we all have **Things to Do**. Furthermore, to the extent that we make this book acceptable and understandable to a broader audience, we fail to authentically reflect who Dad is, was, and will be.

There is a bias in the selection of material. I am here, while my brother and sister are not. I have asked Dad to include many of my favorite stories and the result is too few about Rick, Dor, Mother, and many others. Those will have to await Volume Two.

A few technical notes are in order:

- some names and other insignificant details have been omitted or modified in order to protect, in Dad's words, "the guilty parties."
- In honor of Laplace, Fourier, and other transforms used in Physics, **BAD WORDS** have been transformed using a Caesar Shift Code with Shift Value three (Google it, if necessary).
- Perhaps stemming from his study of German at Carleton College, Dad always has used **Excessive Capitalization**. While many editorial hours have been wasted attempting to standardize this aspect of the book, there is ultimately no system for which words are capitalized or not.
- Despite having an English major as his Mother, Dad never has been able to spell korecktlee. In a few cases (blond) we

---

[3] And collecting money for funding endowed scholarships.
[4] There is almost nothing from the late 60's when the family lived in Ann Arbor and Rochester, New York.

have allowed Fritz's best misspellings to stand. In a few others (Crockadilians) we have footnoted his unique variants.

- Comments, criticisms, and complaints about this book would be greatly appreciated. Please send to freddolittle@gmail.com.

Dad (and Mφm), it was wonderful growing up in this family. We all love you and want to preserve some sense of who you are for as long as possible. May God continue to bless you with **SIGNIFICANT THINGS TO DO** here on this planet, and forevermore.

With love,

Freddy the Editor
August 14, 2015

Part I. Childhood Family Stories (1933-1939)

1. Uncle Maurice and Aunt Peg

My Uncle, Maurice Flower Johnson, was a graduate of Ferris Institute of Technology in the class of 1899. He proceeded to Michigan Agricultural College (now Michigan State University or "Moo U"), earned a Master's Degree in Something, and joined the Department of Mathematics and Engineering.

There were just two Professors[5] in the department in those days and Engineering was mostly Civil Engineering, including Surveying, Municipal water systems, Designing Buildings, etc. Eventually the College added two faculty and split the Department into a Department of Mathematics and a Department of Engineering. There was no such thing as Electrical Engineering, Electronic Engineering or Automotive Engineering.

Uncle Maurice eventually resigned his faculty appointment to work on the construction of the ***Panama Canal***. My Mother told me Uncle Maurice caught Yellow Fever, but my sister says it was Malaria. He came home and after two years finally recovered from whatever the disease was.

---

[5] Dr. Phelps studied German in School and it seems to have led him into a lifelong habit of **Excessive Capitalization**, especially of Nouns. While much editing effort has gone towards Increasing Consistency in this publication, every effort has been made to preserve the Spirit of Fritz's capitalization habits.

By the time I was old enough to know who Uncle Maurice was, he was teaching Mathematics at Northern Montana University in Havre, Montana. Once in a while Aunt Peg would load her three children into their Model A Ford, and drive to Grand Rapids to visit her Mother (my Grandmother, Rose Bush).

One day when I was about six years old, I was standing on the side porch of Grandmother's house in Grand Rapids with my Mother. She looked at the sun's position and said "It is about three in the afternoon, but where Aunt Peg lives, it is only noon."

What an astonishing thing to say!!! Naturally I wanted to know why? How could it possibly be three in the afternoon in Grand Rapids, and noon in Montana? Mom said Dad would have to show me when he got home.

We had a single light bulb over the kitchen sink. Dad told me to pretend that it was the Sun. Then he used an orange and said "Pretend this is the earth. You can see that only one side is illuminated, and the other side is dark."

Then he rotated the orange to show me how the sun can "come up" in the morning and "go down" at night. Then he showed how the axis of rotation of the Earth is tipped, and by walking in a big circle, tried to show how the days are shorter in the winter, and longer in the summer. Of course the circle was only half there, because the wall the sink was on prevented him from completing the circle. But it was a fascinating lesson in any case.

Some weeks later, there was an eclipse of the moon, and using the same lightbulb, Dad showed me how the earth casts a shadow, and if things line up right, you can see the shadow on the moon. But usually the moon misses the earth's shadow as it revolves around the earth every 27.3 days.

Aunt Peg told me that they had rattlesnakes in Montana and how they would buzz their tails before they try to kill you with a poisonous bite. I thought it would be nice to have a real rattlesnake skin and a rattle. I gave her one of Grandmother's mousetraps and asked her to catch one for me when she got back to Montana. I had seen how a mousetrap caught a mouse and killed him and why wouldn't it work on a rattlesnake as well?

Several months later a cardboard box addressed to **ME** arrived in the mail. When I opened it, I found a rattlesnake skin and a rattle! The rattle was fun, and I would sneak up behind my sister and rattle it, causing her to scream. Of course I got punished for scaring my sister, but it was well worth it.

2. Curtis, Michigan

A. The Cardboard Clothes

My Father had severe Hay Fever, and he always wanted his two weeks of vacation in August. He would rent a cabin from a Frenchman named Heine La Clarke on Manistique Lake, near Curtis, Michigan.

A rowboat was part of the rental agreement, and we would pull it out of the water onto two saplings, which Heine had attached to the dock. Of course I could never remember that they were slippery, and I would try to walk on them, but I always fell into the lake.

One day my Mother had put dry clothes on me so many times, everything I had was on the line drying. So naturally I tried to walk on the saplings one more time, and I got thoroughly soaked. With no dry clothes to put on, I did the next best thing and put on a cardboard box! What I did not know was, that if you read it carefully, the box has printed on it, "Keep in a Dry Place." Mother took a photograph which has generated many hearty laughs over the last $3/4^{ths}$ of a Century.

B. THE FIRE

One evening Mom was washing dishes after dinner and looked out of the window over the sink and saw a huge wall of flames. At her scream, Dad came running and started to throw everything we owned into suitcases. They were so full, they would not close. No problem; he just took off his belt, and used it to cinch up the first suitcase. Whereupon he took it to the far end of the dock, ready to throw it into the rowboat if the fire spread.

I was so shaken up by all this, I rescued only a large glass salt shaker that cost Dad exactly 3 cents, by running to the dock and putting it next to the suitcase.

Dad eventually walked up the two track to see what was burning. It was Heine's barn. Fortunately, Heine had discovered the fire before it had spread significantly, and had let his cows and horses and pigs out, thus saving their lives.

The fire was caused by **spontaneous combustion of hay** that was not dry enough to put in the barn. Several nearby neighbors and Dad fought the fire all night long. For several hours, Dad pumped water from a well for the other men to use. He was pretty tired the next morning after being up all night.

C. THE MODEL T

Heine had a Model T Ford which his father liked to drive to the tavern in Curtis. He only wanted to do this if he had already had a little too much wine at dinner. A Model T had to be **hand cranked** to start, and when Heine's Dad was a little drunk, the darn car would never start. He never learned that Heine put a **potato into the exhaust pipe**, which increased the back Pressure in the motor, preventing the car from starting. But the next day, the darn car would start on the first or second crank! I learned several good lessons that day:

- A Model T had to be hand cranked to start it.

- Wet Hay will heat up by itself and catch fire, so it must remain in the field to dry, before it is put in a barn or silo.
- I learned about spontaneous combustion.
- Engines have back Pressure, even if I did not know what it meant.
- I learned what getting drunk meant.

D. THE FOREST FIRE

I think the last time we went to Curtis was in 1939. We were in a new cabin that Heine had just built. One day we saw a long line of Civilian Conservation Corps (CCC) Boys, each carrying a back pack Indian Pump with five gallons of water and a shovel, or a thing like a hoe, with a saw tooth edge.

They were on their way to fight a forest fire a few miles to the West. It must have been a small fire, because we could not see any smoke in the distance. They sat down along the path they were following for a five minute rest, and upon command, all jumped to attention and continued their long hike. It was awesome to watch them snake along the trail until they finally disappeared from sight.

Part II. School Days (1938-1951)

3. Kindergarten Assignment – Draw a Picture of a Ship

I do not remember the name of the Teacher, but it might have been Mrs. Quigley who told us to draw a picture of a naval ship on a huge sheet of paper that was taped to the wall of the classroom. I tried to draw a battleship, but I am not a very good Artist, and the ship looked sort of lopsided. Mrs. Quigley wanted to know why I had drawn a huge fire in the middle of the ship.

Isn't it obvious, a battleship needs lots of steam to make it go and so you need a fire to make the steam? I had no idea how the steam was used, but my Uncle Bub was an Engineering Officer in the Navy in World War I and had tried to explain it to me. Of course I did not really understand it much, but I knew he was responsible for the huge fires that made all the steam that made all the machinery work.

I do not remember whether Mrs. Quigley was impressed or not, but I did not have to put the fire out. No other little kid in my class had a fire in his ship so how could it go through the water? I never did learn what propelled those ships and how anyone could be so dumb as to have no means of propulsion! I have often wondered whether Mrs. Quigley thought some day in the future, I would be a Naval Officer (E).[6] If she did, I failed, but I did become a grunt in the Army Chemical Corps, making it all the way up to Private First Class.

---

[6] A standard abbreviation for "Engineer."

4. Third Grade Math – Multiplication

Math was always the fun class in School and third grade was no exception, but the 3rd Grade Teacher was lacking a few smarts. She insisted that 2 x 3 = 6 was exactly the same as 3 x 2 = 6 which is clearly ridiculous because 2 x 3 = 3 + 3 and 3 x 2 = 2 + 2 + 2. That is, multiplication is a fast way to make multiple additions and only a moron would say that 3 + 3 is the same thing as 2 + 2 + 2.

Naturally this caused a note to be sent to Fritz's Mother explaining that her Son was discourteous, rude, impolite and had no manners. Fritz had no concept of commuting arithmetic, but Mom, who was an English major, could see his logic and it was clear that the Teacher was a dimwit. Fritz did not deserve any punishment, although he could have been more diplomatic in expressing his opinion of the Teacher. This was a good lesson, and prevented this bad little boy from suggesting that future Teachers had brains that could only be observed with a microscope.[7] Lesson learned, but not the one intended!

5. Fourth Grade Math – Long Division

In trying to teach long division, a good way for a Teacher to not endear herself to a small boy is by cancelling Math class for the day. It was, in fact, the **Most Awful Day** in the history of School. Fritz was not about to take this insult lightly and stomped up to the Teacher's desk and demanded that **SHE ASSIGN MATH PROBLEMS, BECAUSE IT WAS CLEARLY UNFAIR,**[8] **AND A TERRIBLE SIN TO BOOT,**

---

[7] A claim contradicted in the 8th grade math story.
[8] The original document has "**UNFARE.**"

TO CANCEL THE ONLY FUN CLASS OF THE DAY. He was told, "Go make up at least 50 long division problems and solve them." After making up and solving probably more than 100 problems (but after all these years I have forgotten the exact number), I again stomped up to the Teacher's desk and demanded that she grade them.

Isn't it common knowledge that Teachers grade Math papers all night long? What else could she possibly do for fun? Television was not invented yet, and it would take a half century for Fritz to learn that trying to set a Guinness World Record for Cocker Spaniel petting probably was not an option either. Laughing at a Student who wanted his problems graded did not sit too well with Fritz. But such is life: "we just have to grin and bear it."

6. Eighth Grade Math – Mrs. McGregor and Baseball

When Mrs. McGregor taught us about squares she was very clear; a square must have four right angles and the four line segments must have equal lengths, and the important thing is that the opposite sides are parallel. That is to say, the line segment between home plate and 1st base and the line segment from 2nd to 3rd base should be parallel and equal in length, and the side between 1st base and 2nd base and the line from 3rd base to home must also be parallel and equal in length. But clearly this is false – the line from home to 1st is antiparallel to the line from 2nd to 3rd. Poor Mrs. McGregor did not know parallel from antiparallel!

Next, Mrs. McGregor committed an unpardonable sin. She decided to take us outside and teach us how to play baseball (as if boys in the 8th grade did not know how to play baseball)! She declared that baseball is played on a ***diamond*** which has four right angles and four sides of equal length. Two of these sides just happen to be parallel (really antiparallel) to each other and the other pair of sides also just happens to be (anti)parallel to each other, but one of the pairs is perpendicular to the other pair.

The day was a little blustery, but so what. We had had a good day so far, but when Mrs. McGregor carefully explained that a baseball **diamond** had four right angles and that the diamond also had four sides of equal length and furthermore, the sides were parallel if you only took two of them at a time (and you had better figure out which two that was), it started to smell like a limburger cheese sandwich[9] which had been left on a fence post in the sun too long. A glance clearly showed that we were playing baseball on a **square**!

But Mrs. McGregor clearly did not know parallel lines from antiparallel lines, or that the playing field was really an equiangular rhombus. Tragedy! Mrs. McGregor was no smarter than that dunce of a Third Grade Teacher who thought 3 x 2 was exactly the same as 2 x 3. A note once more went home explaining that it was not nice to suggest that even an electron microscope would fail to show the size of Mrs. McGregor's brain.

Mother just laughed when she was told that an electron microscope could see things on a scale of Ångströms and that one Ångström was 10^{-10} meters, so a cubic Ångström had a volume of 10^{-30} m^3, which set an upper limit for the size of Mrs. McGregor's brain. Mother had long since learned that it was useless to try to explain to her Son that Grade School Marms[10] are remarkably deficient in knowledge of

---

[9] According to Wikipedia, "In the early 20th century, Limburger sandwiches became a popular lunch for working people due to their affordability and nutritious qualities."

[10] The Wiktionary says: (US, slang) A woman who is a teacher, especially a teacher in a schoolhouse; may carry the connotation she is severe. "The schoolmarm, running the old west one-room school, is a stock character in western movies."

any kind, and especially deficient in knowledge of Mathematics!!! Why on earth did the School Board keep such dunces on the teaching staff?

However, I will give Mrs. McGregor credit for teaching us that adverbs must end in "ly" and that a preposition must always be followed by the object of the preposition. It was several years later when Fritz was in the Army, on furlough, and driving through Massachusetts, that he noticed that road signs said, "Drive Slow**ly**, Thick**ly** Settled." I suppose that the Commissioner of the Highway Department was a graduate of that wannabe Cambridge University (President Kennedy's Alma Mater)[11] and insisted that all road signs be written in proper English. Indeed I am properly impressed with Mrs. McGregor's English, but not her Mathematics.

7. Freshman Year in High School – The Ultimate Carpenter

I was a freshman in High School in 1947 and first semester took a class from Mr. Sartwell on Mechanical Drawing. He showed us many drawings he had made in his younger days. They were all dated 1901, 1902, or 1903 and were still in good shape 40 years later. Second semester I took a class in wood shop from Mr. Dunlop, and towards the end of the semester we were told to design and make a piece of furniture.

I chose to make a night stand which was about 30 cm wide x 30 cm deep x 40 cm high. It had a curved top shelf which I designed to hold a Crosley Tube Radio,[12] which I did not own. Transistors would be

---

[11] Kennedy graduated from Harvard University in 1940.
[12] Wikipedia: "By 1924, Crosley Radio Corporation was the largest radio manufacturer in the world."

invented several years in the future. The mass of my virtual radio would have been considerably less than 1.0 kg. I proceeded to manufacture the night stand, but it had no legs, and so Mr. Dunlop told me to design some legs for it and to make them. In order to make them strong enough I chose to make the legs out of 4x4 inch timbers attached to hefty rails using tongue and groove joints held together with hot hide glue.

Mr. Dunlop did not approve my design for the legs, but later that day Mr. Sartwell came to the woodshop and I saw the two Teachers looking with interest at my design. Then Mr. Sartwell started to laugh and I was summoned to Mr. Dunlop's desk. When I got there Mr. Dunlop asked me what I intended to put on my night stand.

"A Crosley Radio, Sir."

Mr. Dunlop replied, "Do you think the legs will be strong enough to hold it up?" I was too stupid to notice the sarcasm and answered, "Well, I suppose I could use 6x6 timbers for the legs if you think I need it!"

That caused gales of laughter. After things had quieted down it was suggested that I might want to redesign the legs unless, of course, I was expecting to entertain an Elephant in my bedroom, and provide him with a chair to sit on.

Years later, when I was a Student at Carleton, my Mother sent me a cartoon she cut out of the Spokane paper. It was about a Handyman who had built a chair and reinforced the rungs, which were made of 2x4's, with heavy-duty angle iron. The caption was the Woodworker's Wife talking to a friend and saying, "Well one thing you can say, Fritz makes sturdy furniture." I kept that cartoon for decades, but somehow it has disappeared. I do not remember seeing it since we moved to Mount Pleasant in 1970. Tragedies are part of my life.

8. War in Mr. Sartwell's Class

Each Student in Mr. Sartwell's class had his own drawing table and we were paired side by side with another Student. My table was in the second row and some **Idiot** sat in front of me in the first row. I took great pains with my drawings and after each drawing in pencil I traced all lines with India ink using my drawing instruments: a T-Square and Triangle. **Idiot Boy** was not too pleased that I always got a much better grade than he did. One day he brought a squirt gun to class, and, as I was finishing several days of work, he squirted both my drawing and me which caused the India ink to run, ruining my drawing. Mr. Sartwell saw **Idiot Boy's** attack, but said nothing.

Mother had used a large rubber bulb syringe to blow wax out of my ear a few weeks earlier, so when I got home I searched for the bulb until I found it and put it in my pocket. It was fully loaded with cold water from the drinking fountain before I entered class the next day. **Idiot Boy** decided to squirt me again because he had had so much fun the previous day. Out came the ear syringe. I put it on my desk and mashed it using my full weight on both hands. The deluge that hit **Idiot Boy** was awesome! Of course **Idiot Boy** let out a shriek and Mr. Sartwell started to laugh while **Idiot Boy** was thoroughly drenched from head to foot.

I do not recall that **Idiot Boy** squirted a drawing of mine again. Perhaps he thought I would bring ice to School so that the water would be good and cold if I needed to defend myself again. Actually I was prepared for a third attack and my ammunition would have been a **FULL BOTTLE of black India Ink**. Fortunately, I did not have to use the **INK** in my syringe, but it would have made a wonderful mess, and **Idiot Boy** would have had a scrub bath **WITH A STEEL BRISTLED BRUSH**.

9. High School Algebra and Haydn's Creation

In 1947, Lewis and Clark High School hired Mr. Wuhman as a Teacher of Algebra. He had just returned from a tour of duty in the Philippines as a sailor on a PT Boat,[13] but he proved he was no smarter than our 3rd Grade Teacher or our 8th Grade Teacher when the topic was logarithms. We learned how to look up the mantissa (decimal part) of the logarithm in a log table and figure out the characteristic (integer part) by ourselves. It was fun to learn how to turn multiplication or division problems into addition or subtraction problems using four place or five place mantissa tables.

Then my Dad gave me a book by Professor Glover that he had used in his Accounting classes at the University of Michigan containing ***Seven Place Logarithms of Numbers From 1 to 100,000***. He had worn out the binding in his Accounting classes and I had to pay $8.00 to have it rebound. I still have it. Then I made the serious mistake of asking Mr. Wuhman how the numbers in the log table were calculated. He did not know! Then I asked why logarithms worked the way he told us they did. He did not know that either. His standard answer, no matter what question I asked him was, "Don't ask so many questions; just do what I tell you to do. It works like I said it would because it is easier to add and subtract than it is to multiply or divide."

Just a minute! "Because it is easier to add or subtract" is the reason it works? A very unsatisfactory answer if I had ever heard one!!! Poor Mr. Wuhman, surely all his smarts were fried in the sun while he was a sailor boy. So then I discovered that we were using "logarithms to the base 10" called "common logarithms" and that there were also logarithms

---

[13] A PT boat (short for Patrol Torpedo boat) was a torpedo-armed fast attack craft used by the United States Navy in World War II.

to the base e called "natural logarithms," but Mr. Wuhman said we would only use base 10 logs. He had no idea why anyone would ever use base e logs and he certainly did not know anything about e. This revelation reinforced the idea that Mr. Wuhman had spent too much time in the Philippines in the sun without his pith helmet.[14]

It took me a long time to figure out that, in using base ten logs, we were simply replacing any number with 10 raised to a decimal fractional power. To wit,

$$2 = 10^{0.30103}$$

and

$$8 = 10^{0.90309}$$

and then 2×8 is obtained by just adding the exponents:

$$2 * 8 = 10^{0.30103} * 10^{0.90309} = 10^{1.20412}.$$

Then we can use the log table backwards to find the antilog of $10^{1.20412}$, which, as any fool knows, is just 16. So the problem is to figure out how to obtain the fractional exponents!!! It is not too difficult if you know some Calculus, which was invented by Big Isaac[15] in order to make it possible to solve problems that were too hard to do with Algebra or Geometry, but such ideas were far beyond Mr. Wuhman's ken.[16]

Logarithms were invented by John Napier (1550-1617), the Laird[17] of Merchiston, the Scottish Mathematician who also introduced the decimal point, a notation badly needed so that we can express fractions of

---

[14] Wikipedia: The pith helmet (also known as the safari helmet, sun helmet, topee, sola topee, salacot or topi) is a lightweight cloth-covered helmet made of cork or pith, typically pith from the sola, *Aeschynomene aspera*, an Indian swamp plant, or *A. paludosa*, or a similar plant.

[15] Sir Isaac Newton of course.

[16] According to freedictionary.com. Ken: range of knowledge or perception.

[17] From Wikipedia: Laird (/ˈlɛərd/) is a generic name for the owner of a Scottish estate, roughly equivalent to an esquire in England, yet ranking above the same in Scotland.

a number in decimal form, that is, the digits in adjacent columns to the right of the decimal point stand for 1/10, 1/100, 1/1000, etc., just as the digits in the columns to the left of the decimal point stand for multiples of 1, 10, 100, 1000, etc. It is a long, hard job to calculate the fractional exponents for a log table by hand, which is what John Napier had to do, but the finished table allows a person to calculate products or quotients by doing addition or subtraction problems rather than by multiplying by hand, and figuring out the "store" and the "carry" for each pair of digits in the multiplication array, or the inverse in division. Using logs allows a Mathematician to calculate the orbit of a comet in months rather than in years.[18]

Log tables are very useful, as the following example will illustrate. Fritz and Marion[19] went to Warriner Auditorium to hear the CMU[20] Festival Chorus sing Haydn's **Creation**. In the Genesis description of Creation, God tells all the animals to be fruitful and multiply, but surely He did not tell the Adder Snakes how to do this. Obviously they cannot multiply, because they are Adder Snakes.

Fritz figured this during the performance. The Adder Snakes must return to High School and take a course in Wood Shop. After they learn how to make furniture, they can make a *log table* and then use the *log table* to work out the solution to the problem of multiplication.

Someone, who will not be identified, thinks that giggling during a magnificent performance of Haydn's masterpiece is inappropriate, and a smack in the ribs by an elbow does not help the giggling either, especially

---

[18] Editor: And using computers reduces this task to a fraction of a second! One gets the impression that the author regrets the consequences of the invention of the computer.

[19] This woman, otherwise unintroduced to this point, is presumably Fritz's Wife, who indeed goes by that name.

[20] Central Michigan University.

when such a profound truth has been discovered by a mere Professor of Physics Emeritus!

10. High School Chemistry — Why I'm a Physicist and Not a Chemist

There were two Chemistry Teachers in Lewis and Clark High School, Mr. Louderback and Mr. Anderson. My Sister took Chemistry from Mr. Louderback when I was a freshman and she was a junior. She came home one day and was struggling to memorize hundreds of "valences of atoms." I asked her what a valence was and she did not know, but she showed me something about atomic structure and how there are electrons around the nucleus of an atom and how there are shells of electrons. The valence had something to do with how many electrons an atom could snatch away from a neighbor or share with another atom.

Then she showed me a periodic table and the column with Oxygen in it and explained that Oxygen had a valence of -2. So all atoms on the right half of the periodic table apparently had negative valences and the atoms on the left half of the periodic table had positive valences. It looked to me as though a negative valence was just the number of electrons required to completely fill the outer shell of electrons in an atom or the positive valence was just the number of electrons that the atom could donate to another atom. Sure enough Hydrogen had a valence of +1, meaning it can give up one electron. So we checked out a few more atoms and my scheme for determining the valence of an atom seemed to make sense.

Mr. Louderback was stunned the next day when my Sister rattled off the valences of a dozen atoms just by looking at the periodic table. So I determined to have Mr. Anderson when I would take Chemistry in two years as a Junior. I was not about to have a Teacher who made you memorize numbers just to memorize numbers, especially when he did not have any idea what the numbers meant.

It was Mr. Anderson who convinced me to become a Physicist, and he never knew how he did it. It happened this way. He gave us a test one day and one of the questions was "Define a calorie." I wrote, "It is the amount of heat energy needed to raise one gram of water by one degree centigrade." Mr. Anderson gave me a zero for that answer. According to Mr. Anderson, the right answer was "It is the amount heat energy needed to **RAISE THE TEMPERATURE OF** one gram of water by one degree centigrade. If I wanted **TO RAISE ONE GRAM OF WATER** I would have to carry it up a hill!"

That wrinkled old vre[21] was absolutely right and I was wrong! But why didn't he tell us that bit of wisdom in class before the exam??? If I was going to be a Scientist, I would have to learn to be more accurate in everything that I wrote or said, and I had learned by that time that Physics Students always were complaining that they had to be exceedingly precise and careful or they got shot down by Mr. Minard. So it was obvious that it was **PHYSICS** for me and not some sloppy thing like Chemistry. Ah, the lessons you learn in School that the Teacher never knows he is teaching you!

---

[21] In this book, only the Caesar Shift Code transformed forms of **Bad Word**s are published. If you are **Inclined to Be Bad**, shift every letter back three places in the alphabet.

11. High School Physics (1951)

Mr. Minard was the Physics Teacher in Lewis and Clarke High School (LCHS) in Spokane, Washington. It is a shame that we had only one year of High School Physics. Physics was by far the best class offered at LCHS. But in second place would be Miss Clausen's Plane Geometry class, followed by Mr. Kramlich's classes in Solid Geometry, Algebra 3, Algebra 4, and Trigonometry. We had only five sections of Physics in 1950-1951, and Jim Minard, the Son of Mr. Minard, was in my section.

One day Mr. Minard came into class with a sheaf of papers in hand and said, "You have not been doing too well on your homework problems. I have made up 50 extra problems and if you do them I will give you 50 Extra Credit points on your grade. Then he looked at me and said, *"EXCEPT YOU PHELPS! If YOU do them, I will take 50 points OFF your grade!!!"*

HUMMM. CHALLENGE!!!

The next day Mr. Minard asked if anyone had solved the Extra Credit Problems. I looked around and no one raised his hand. So I raised mine and said, "Yes, Mr. Minard, I did." He looked at me a little strangely and said, **"Didn't I till you I would take 50 points off your grade if you did them?"**

"Yes, Mr. Minard, you did."

"Then why on earth did you do them?"

"Well, Mr. Minard, there were three reasons."

"O.K., what is the first reason?"

"Well, Sir, I calculated my grade and decided you could take 50 points off and I would still have enough points for an A for the semester."

A long silence followed. Then, "What was the second reason?"

"Well, Sir, you really didn't think I would give up all that fun did you?"

"So you think doing Physics problems is *FUN*?"

"Oh yes, Sir, the greatest fun in the world!"

"And the third reason?"

"Well, Sir, I wanted you to have the correct key." And I handed him my solutions.

In 2001 I told this story at the 50th High School reunion of the Class of 1951 and Jim Minard spoke up and said, "I remember that day. Very few people got my Dad, but you laid the best job on him he had ever seen. As long as he lived he remembered and spoke of that day every once in a while." It may have been that he was rather proud of the fact that one of his boys had become a Physics Professor. I will have to ask him when I see him in the next life, but when I do, I will not come back and tell you what I learn.

Part III. Carleton College (1951-1955)

12. Why Carleton College?

When I was a very young boy either my Mother or my Father would read to me nearly every day. The stories were fascinating, sometimes from the National Geographic Magazine, once the entire series of the Leather Stocking Tales (five books by James Fenimore Cooper), Charlemagne, King of the Franks, Ivanhoe,…. Often I would have to stop Dad and ask him the meaning of uncommon words like "satiated" or "countenance."

They told me about their professors at the University of Michigan, Bill Payton, Giulio Del Torre, and Lawrence McKinley Gould.

My mother taught me to **NEVER** address as adult by his first name and always use Mr. or Mrs. or Miss, but Dr. Gould was always just Larry to his students. I knew that Larry taught my mother Geology in 1924 and that he was 2nd in Command of Admiral Bird's Antarctic Expedition in 1928.

One day when I was a sophomore in high school, my Father read that Dr. Gould, President of Carleton College, would be preaching at the Congregational Church in Spokane on Sunday. We did not attend church regularly, but he announced that we would all go church to hear Larry. His talk was exciting, but I can no longer remember what it was about.

After the service Mom said, "We must go the narthex and introduce ourselves to Larry." She told him that she was in his Geology class in 1924, but her name was Alice Kellogg in those days. He looked at me and said, "Where are you going to College?"

I answered, "The University of Michigan, of course."

He turned to Mom and said, "**DON'T LET HIM DO IT!**"

Mom thought this was a very odd answer coming from a man who had three degrees from the University of Michigan and who had been Professor of Geology at that institution. Sometime afterwards she wrote him and asked *why* he had said such a thing.

He wrote back stating that if I went to Michigan, for the first two years I would be taught by Graduate Students who were much more interested in their own graduate work than in helping me learn my coursework. On the other hand if I attended a small Liberal Arts College, I would be taught by Senior Professors whose goal was to help me learn the material I was studying and not to publish nonsense in **Prestigious Journals** on a weekly basis just to keep the Dean happy and ensure their next promotion.

After several letters had passed between Spokane and Northfield, Minnesota, she announced that I was going to attend Carleton College. As far as I was concerned, any decision Mom made was set in stone and I would never question it. While I was a high school sophomore I applied for admission to Carleton, and I was promptly admitted to the class of 1955 with a starting date of September 1951.

13. First Year at Carleton

During his senior year in High School, the College advised Fritz that nearly all Students study only one of Math, Chemistry or Physics as a freshman and asked him to choose a discipline. But which one?

It turned out that the Assistant Principal of Lewis and Clarke High School, William W. Taylor, was a graduate of Carleton College, Class of 1931. So Fritz made an appointment to see him and ask which class he should take. Instead of giving him advice, Mr. Taylor got up from his desk and consulted a filing cabinet full of courses taken, grades earned, etc. Upon returning to his desk he said, "Take all three; you can do it."

So in the fall of 1951, Fritz enrolled in Math, Physics, Chemistry, German and English. He had classes from 8 a.m. to noon, six days a week, and Labs from 1 to 5 p.m. on Monday, Wednesday and Friday. It was quite a substantial load of course work for Fritz. Math was pretty simple, Chemistry was fun and Fritz tutored some of the girls in his Chemistry class. They could never figure out how he could do the assigned Chemistry problems for the week in a few minutes. He never told them that he had done the same problem the week before in Physics: After all, the Ideal Gas Laws are the same for Chemistry problems as for Physics problems.

But Physics was a terrible struggle. When he failed the first three Physics hour exams, it was clearly decision time. Physics was by far the most enjoyable class and the decision was easy: "Get Physics or let it get you, and go down with the sinking ship." With the decision made, the question was how to do that? The solution was to close all his other books at 10 p.m. each night and open his Physics book and study as hard as possible until 4 a.m., get three hours of sleep, then, at 7 a.m., get up, eat breakfast and run to the first class of the day, arriving there just as class began.

Eventually, Frau Doktor Blaney noticed that Fritz was not doing very well in German and called him in to her office.

"What do you plan on doing with your life?"

"Be a Physics Professor."

"What are you studying?"

"Physics, Math, Chemistry, German and English."

"How are classes going?"

"Well, Math and Chemistry are fine and I have the Chairman of English for that class and it is going OK, but he told me he would not pass me unless I improved my spelling."

Now it turned out that Dr. Elledge, Chairman of English, had a younger brother, Reese, who was in the Class of 1955 and in the same English class as Fritz. So Fritz asked Reese to read over his required essays and check them for spelling errors. Without letting Dr. Elledge know that Fritz knew who Reese was, he told Dr. Elledge that he had asked someone in the class named Reese to review his spelling, but that the arrangement seemed not to help much. Could Dr. Elledge make any suggestions that might help Fritz improve his spelling?

After this, Dr. Elledge did not mention the spelling problem again. I assume he just gave up on reforming my spelling.

Next, Frau Doktor Blaney asked about class schedules and studying time. She seemed rather stunned to learn had Fritz had classes from 8 a.m. to noon, six days a week, Labs from 1 to 5 p.m. three afternoons a week, followed by six hours/day studying Physics from 10 p.m. to 4 a.m. every night. He just got pooped out before he got around to his German assignments, but he needed German for his language exams in Graduate School!

Frau Doktor was very understanding that Fritz was physically unable to do any more studying than he was already doing and said, "Don't worry about your German. You will have lots of time to work on your German vocabulary when you are in Graduate School."

Fritz did better in German as a sophomore when he chose German Literature of the Nineteenth Century as his literature requirement for his BA Degree.

14. Dean Jarcho

Casey Jarcho, Dean of Men, wanted to see Fritz for some reason and asked him to come to his office during some free period in the morning. But he seemed flabbergasted when Fritz told him he had classes from 8 a.m. to noon, six days a week, but he could come Tuesday or Thursday afternoon, but not Monday, Wednesday or Friday afternoon because they were Lab Days.

It was an interesting visit with Dr. Jarcho because he told Fritz that his Secretary's Husband had had a stroke or heart attack or something while out feeding his pigs and had fallen in the pig pen. Before anyone found him, a good share of him had been eaten by the pigs and he was, of course, quite dead. After 60 years Fritz has no idea why Dean Jarcho wanted to see him or what else they talked about; his RAM seems to be failing! But it was an interesting story about pigs and a good reason to not be a Pig Farmer, so Fritz stuck to Physics!

15. Party and Pressure Politics

Fritz's sophomore, junior and senior years were filled with as many Math and Physics classes as he could squeeze in, but there were a few memorable moments in other classes. As a distribution requirement, Fritz took a course in Party and Pressure Politics from Professor Ralph Fielstad.

A requirement of Professor Fielstad's class was a term paper of not more than ten double spaced typed pages on some topic in Party and Pressure Politics. He gave a suggested list of 120 books that could be read for ideas. Fritz was busy with three Math and Physics classes as well as German Literature of the 19th Century and certainly did not have time to read one book, let alone 120, so what to do?

After stewing[22] about the matter for a few days, the solution was obvious:[23] Write a paper about ten ways to improve the electoral process

---

[22] i.e., mulling.

with changes designed to help the Republicans and hurt the Democrats[24]. Fritz cannot remember many of the details but one Brilliant Idea was that the people who pay the bills should have more say on how the money is wasted by the Federal Government than people who pay less. All men and women get one vote, but you get one additional vote if you **PAY** any income tax at all. In addition you get one additional vote for each $1000 dollars of tax you pay. There would be no limit on the number of votes you could receive: if you paid income tax of one million dollars, you would get 1002 votes! And if you file a joint return with your Wife, she also gets 1002 votes. There were nine other wonderful suggestions, but Fritz cannot remember what they were. Such are the ravages of time.

After Professor Fielstad graded the papers he selected two to read to the class. One was Fritz's and one by someone else. He declared that Fritz's paper was one of the most original and creative he had ever read, and it was written by a Physics major, not a Political Science major!!!

After he read the second paper, he announced that the author had been expelled and would never graduate from Carleton College. Fritz thought the second paper was rather well written and informative, and raised his hand. He told Professor Fielstad that is sounded like a great paper, so why was the author expelled?

Professor Fielstad agreed that it was a well written paper but the author was expelled for plagiarism because it was copied verbatim from the Encyclopedia Britannica and the cheater forgot to check the initials of

---

[23] Physicists (and Mathematicians) are so enamored of their own intelligence that after struggling mightily and finally solving a difficult problem they will typically exclaim, "Oh, yes. Now I see. It really is obvious after all."

[24] Fritz, from birth, was raised to be a Republican. His Father trained their dog so that when the dog was asked, "Would you rather be a Democrat or a **Dead Dog**?" the dog would roll over and stick her four paws in the air.

the author, **RF, RALPH FIELSTAD. The Student had copied the Professor's own article!!!**

16. THE MOUSE IN BURTON HALL

When I was a junior in Carleton College, I roomed with Obert Undem on the 4th floor of Burton Hall. It was hot up there, so hot in fact that we often slept on top of our beds with only pajama pants on and no sheet or pajama top of any kind. One night Obert was up rather late studying Greek and I had given up studying Physics and gone to sleep. Eventually Obert gave up and went to bed and was fast asleep when he was rudely awakened by a blood curdling scream from his previously snoring roommate!

A MOUSE HAD RUN ACROSS FRITZ'S BARE CHEST AND AWAKENED HIM! That mouse was as scared of the scream as Obert was and ran up the back wall of Obert's closet and got his head stuck between the shelf near the top of the closet and the rear wall. The walls were concrete blocks, so it was good footing for a mouse.

A few days later a rather sickening stink seemed to be growing in our room. When Obert was in Greek class, Fritz looked a little to see if he could find the source of the stink, but no luck. When Obert returned from class, Fritz suggested that it was time to wash his underwear because he thought the stink was coming from Obert's closet! Then Fritz went off to a Physics Lab and Obert took over the investigation and found the mouse who was thoroughly ripe and beginning to liquefy.

So what did Obert do? He held *Fritz's* waste basket in place pulled out the shelf enough to let the mouse fall out of its prison. After Fritz emptied[25] **HIS** waste basket **HE SCRUBBED IT OUT FOR AN**

HOUR WITH SOAP AND HOT WATER, but he does not remember whether he took the waste basket into the shower with him, or if he used the huge sink in the Janitor's closet. Fritz's *RAM* is not as good as it was when he was a wee laddie. Or has he just developed a bad case of galloping senility?

---

[25] Spelled "emptyied" in the inspired original.

Part IV. Summer in Los Alamos (1955)

17. Before There Were Calculators

I graduated from College in June, 1955 and enrolled, starting in the fall, in Physics at the Horace H. Rackham School of Graduate Studies at the University of Michigan. During the summer I worked at Los Alamos Scientific Laboratory near Santa Fe, New Mexico. That is the place where a thousand Physicists, Chemists, Engineers, and all kinds of Technicians; including many foreigners like Enrico Fermi, Niels Bohr and Edward Teller designed and built Fat Man and Little Boy, the two Atomic Bombs that ended World War II.

In 1955 the Lab was getting ready for some tests of Hydrogen Bombs at Bikini Atoll and my job was to calibrate a Xenon Micro Flash Lamp to be used in calibrating our equipment. We obtained a lot of experimental data and I used an IBM 501 tube computer for several complicated computations. Los Alamos had three of these 501 computers and each came with four full-time Engineers who did preventive maintenance for four hours every day, starting at midnight.

The memory was a large rack of cathode ray tubes such as you would have had for a picture tube for a viewing screen in a Television Set in those Neanderthal Days. I learned new prefixes such as "nano" ($= 10^{-9}$) and "pico" ($= 10^{-12}$), but could not use them outside the Lab because they were top secret, and if a **Russian Spy** learned about them, it would surely tell him something he wanted to know about Atomic Bombs. Somehow these prefixes started appearing in every freshman Physics book published since 1970 and no one seems too worried that some **Russian Spy** would drop an H-bomb on us because he has learned some standard shorthand from his Pre-Med Physics class.

The neatest thing in the computer room was a wooden case with a glass window and a small hammer hanging from it by a chain. The case contained a 12 or 15 column Abacus and a large wooden sign below it which read, "**IN CASE OF EMERGENCY SMASH GLASS**." I never had to smash the glass, but it gave me an idea. I constructed an Abacus using three knitting needles and faucet washers, which I used for adding up grades in the fall when I was a Teaching Fellow at Michigan!!!

I had to teach several office mates how it worked. It might have caused me to file for bankruptcy because it probably cost me 25 cents for parts but I really do not remember, perhaps because that was 57 years ago and my memory is failing. Don't laugh, Texas Instruments had not yet invented the hand-held calculator. We used log tables if an accuracy of five significant digits was satisfactory or slide rules for all our Physics problems if we only needed three significant digits.

18. The 18 Kilogram Watermelon

The Lab allowed summer Students to live in a barracks which had many tiny individual rooms and a large community kitchen. The nearest grocery store was a Safeway, several blocks away. If you did not have a car, you had to carry your groceries back to the barracks. I had gone there to buy food for a week, and found a huge watermelon which rang nicely when tapped by a knuckle, indicating it was full of juice and should be sweet.

When I came out of the store, several of the guys who lived in the same barracks were there, starting the walk home. I had a very heavy load, and asked if anyone would carry a bag for me? No luck, so I struggled home with my two enormous bags.

They all cooked their dinners, and I cooked and ate mine. Then I fetched the watermelon, and started to cut it open. They all said, "We want a piece too."

I said, "Too bad. No one would help me carry it home, so I shall eat the whole thing by myself." To taunt them a little further, I ate each bite slowly and deliberately, and it took me about two hours to finish the melon, which, at 4 cents a pound, had cost me $1.60.

When I finished, they all said, "We didn't think you could do it!!!" I cannot remember how many trips I made to the bathroom that night, but I learned that my kidneys were working just fine, so it was not a wasted evening after all.

19. Spaghetti

When I lived at home, Mom never made spaghetti, but we had it once in a while at Carleton. I loved it, and decided to try to cook some at Los Alamos. The first attempt was pretty bad, so I wrote my Mom and asked for recipes. She wrote back, "All you need is a little bit of courage to try new things."

O.K! I decided to learn how to make good spaghetti sauce and I **would make it every night until I learned the secret**. I had spaghetti every evening for dinner, for **40 days in a row**. Each night it was a little better than the day before.

My final recipe was 200 grams of hamburger, a large onion and half a green pepper, both cut into small pieces, all thrown into the meat and cooked, while I added a can of Campbell's Tomato soup, and a large amount of Heinz catsup for flavoring, and a small can of mushrooms. The last thing was to cook 100 grams of spaghetti and then have a **Feast Fit for a King**.

I must say that after 40 days of spaghetti, I was happy to have something else for dinner, which, if I remember correctly, was a white sauce cooked with cut-up dried beef and then poured on mashed potatoes.

Part V. Graduate School, Take One (1955-1956)

20. Sinking Independently with Kasimir Fajans

Classes at Michigan were great. I had courses in Intermediate Differential Equations (Carleton had no course in Differential Equations) and Fourier Series. I had Professor Dennison for Classical Mechanics, Professor Dushnick for Functions of a Complex Variable and Professor Uhlenbeck for Thermodynamics. You may remember Professor Uhlenbeck because he and his classmate Goudsmit were the guys that gave the electron a Spin Quantum Number to explain the splitting of spectral lines in a magnetic field.

Then there was Kasimir Fajans,[26] Professor of Chemistry. He was Professor Bunsen's last Ph.D. Student (you got it, the guy who invented the Bunsen burner). He had been Der Herr Doktor Professor of Chemistry at the University of Berlin, which was about as high as any German Professor could go. But he was a Jew, and one day after he had gone to the University, a friend came to him with his passport and some money and told him that the Gestapo was going to arrest him that night, and he would be dead by morning because he would resist arrest and they would shoot him.

So the friend said, "Follow your usual routine this morning. Go to lunch at the usual time, but go in the front door of the café and straight

---

[26] Editor's note: His name was spelled "Cassimere Fijans" in the original document and Google searches were insufficient to establish his correct identity. In the end, I was able to determine his name based on Fajans' reported use of the word "quanticule," as discussed below.

out the back door to the train station and take the train. That will get you across the German border in the minimum time." I think he may have headed for Denmark. Just after his train crossed the border the Nazis erected saw horses, closing the border to stop any more trains.

Professor Fajans was an interesting character; he was always sucking in his false teeth and then he would point a finger in the air and say, "I vant you boys to sink independently." We would all respond, "Vee are sinking independently, Professor Fajans," and then we would laugh. He could never figure out why we were laughing.

One day I nearly caused Professor Fajans to have a stroke or a heart attack. He was explaining how atoms can be stuck to each other to make molecules by inserting electrons (he called them "quanticules," and used a dot for a quanticule) between adjacent atoms and he used CO_2 as his example. I asked him how quanticules differed from Linus Pauling's[27] chemical bonds.

WRONG QUESTION! He went into a ***towering rage*** and shouted that Pauling had stolen his idea and renamed the quanticules "chemical bonds" and used a line to represent them instead of a dot. Then he explained how Lord Rayleigh had undercut him with the discovery of Argonne and he (**THE GREAT PROFESSOR FAJANS**) should have been given credit for discovering the Noble Gasses in the Periodic Table instead of Lord Rayleigh.

He was a little friendlier after I apologized for asking the wrong question and upsetting him. He seemed to think that I should have known about the Noble Gases and quanticules. But there was nothing in American Textbooks about quanticules, and, naturally, Lord Rayleigh got a Nobel Prize for discovering Argonne[28] **BECAUSE** he was an

---

[27] Pauling won the Nobel Prize in Chemistry in 1954 and, as of the year 2000, according to Wikipedia, was considered the "16th most important scientist in history."

Englishman, and the Nobel Committee always favored Englishmen or Americans over Germans.

21. Thermodynamics

One of the Students in Thermodynamics was one of Fritz's office mates, Howard Bryant, who was best man at Fritz's wedding a couple years later. Howard had taken Thermodynamics at Berkeley as an undergraduate and thought his class notes looked quite familiar. After class one day the two Students stopped to talk to Professor Uhlenbeck and Howie asked him if he knew Professor so and so at Berkeley. The answer was immediate.

"Ja, sure; he vas von of mine Graduate Students!" Uhlenbeck added, "Vell, I got de notes from Lorentz[29], und Lorentz got de notes from Gibbs.[30] In fact dhey are Gibbs' original notation. Dhey are straight from de horses' mouth!"

"I thought so; the class notes look pretty familiar."

---

[28] Rayleigh won the Nobel Prize in Physics in 1904.
[29] That is Hendrik Lorenz who won the Nobel Prize in 1902.
[30] Gibbs (1839-1903) was a pioneer in Thermodynamics. According to Wikipedia he was, "an American scientist who made important theoretical contributions to physics, chemistry, and mathematics."

Part VI. The Army Years (1956-1958)

22. Don't Never

I finished my first year of Graduate School and secured a summer job as Junior Engineer at Texas Instruments in Dallas. They assigned me to study the spectral response characteristics of their newly invented Photo-transistor. I found a place to stay with an Old Lady who had a room to rent. I cannot even remember her name, but she had a Son-in-Law who was a grizzled Old Sergeant with about 35 years of service in the Army. After a month on the job, my Mom forwarded a letter to me from President Eisenhower. **IT WAS A DRAFT NOTICE.**

The Old Sergeant was at the house the day I received the letter. I showed it to him and he said, "Youz a nice guy. I'm gonna give youz a little advice and if ya takes it, it'll help keep ya outta trouble. **DON'T NEVER VOLUNTEER FER NUTHIN.**" I rather liked the Old Sergeant and I took his advice many times. And so I reported for duty as directed and entered the U.S. Army as a Buck Private.

23. Into the Army

And so it came about that Fritz raised his right hand at the Dallas Court House and was inducted into the U.S. Army near the end of June, 1956. The new Soldiers were put on a bus and taken to Fort Hood, Texas where they were issued wool uniforms. It was extremely hot outside. Then they were pretty well stripped of most of their clothing and both arms were used as pin cushions, receiving about 50 inoculations. I am sure we had shots for every tropical illness you could think of: Typhoid Fever, Cholera, Yellow Fever, Dengue Fever, … , and a whole bunch I could not even guess. At the end of the line both arms felt like you had encountered a porcupine who didn't particularly like your eye color or some other infantile defect. Then they put us on a train to Fort Bliss in El Paso, all the way across Texas.

Something gave me a high fever and after dinner in the dining car I could not get into my assigned Pullman birth for the night trip to Fort Bliss. The other guys were as weak as I was and it took five of them to push me into my bunk. I needed to go to the bathroom in the middle of the night but did not dare to get out of bed for fear that I would have no place to sit, let alone sleep, if I could not get back into bed by myself. I was a Very Happy Private when the Conductor finally showed up at six in the morning and told us to report for breakfast as soon as possible because we were not that far from El Paso.

Fort Bliss is certainly a misnomer. It was hotter than khoo[31], about 107 on Fahrenheit's scale or about 41.6 on Celsius' scale. After receiving our uniforms and boots we were lined up outside the barracks, marched to the Quartermaster's store and each given three wool blankets. Why did we need three blankets if it was so hot on the Parade Ground? The Sergeant said, "Just wait until the middle of the night and you will see why!" High desert with no humidity cools down extremely rapidly as soon as the sun goes down. And it was COLD in the barracks, even with all the gas heaters running flat out.

The next morning we were ordered out to the Parade Ground and a Sergeant asked if anyone could Type. A whole bunch of guys volunteered, but not I: I thought it best to obey the Old Sergeant's advice and wait to see what was going to happen. After the Sergeant got as many

---

[31] The key to decrypting **Bad Words** is explained in the footnote in the story "High School Chemistry."

men as he wanted, he shouted, "Yooz Guys look like da Type! Left Face!" and off they marched.

They dragged back to the barracks after we had had supper and they were all pooped out. I asked one of the guys what happened to them. He said, "You wouldn't believe it; we carried typewriters all day from one warehouse to another." How they managed in wool uniforms with outside temperature well above 40 Celsius I don't know. But one guy had a heat stroke, and when the medics got to him, he was dead. He was from Alaska. **YUP, DON'T NEVER VOLUNTEER FER NUTHIN!**

24. The Professor

A few days later we were issued cotton uniforms which were better in the heat. Basic training was a series of pushups and jumping jacks and running long distances until we were so sore we could hardly move. We started with one pushup and each day added one more until eventually we could do about 60. It was interesting to see how much stronger we became over the course of two months.

It was not long before the 200 boys in Fritz's company started calling him "Professor." Possibly this was because the Sergeants asked a lot of questions, and when nobody could provide a decent answer, the Professor was asked because usually he could figure out the answer wanted by the Sergeant.

One question Fritz distinctly remembers answering was why, when you are sighting-in a rifle, and the shots are consistently hitting the target to the right of the bull's-eye, do you have to move the peep site to the left?

Think of tying a string from the front site to the rear site and then moving the back site to the left. The effect is to rotate the rifle about the back site, and you must have the two sights lined up so your shot goes where the string is pointing. Fritz never did learn whether the Sergeant did not know that, or perhaps it had just never been explained to him in a way he could understand. But he seemed to get it that time.

25. When to Volunteer

I did violate the Old Sergeant's rule about a year later. I had been assigned to the Chemical Corps and was stationed at the U.S. Army Chemical Center[32] in Edgewood, Maryland. We had Training every Saturday morning. One Saturday the Sergeant in charge of training asked for 150 volunteers to police the grounds (pick up cigarette butts and small scraps of paper), but no one moved.

After repeating his order several times I saw another Sergeant counting the troops that were arrayed in the street in front of him. I did a quick count and decided that our four companies numbered about 800 Soldiers and concluded that the Sergeant was going to ask for 650 volunteers to police the post. Sure enough, pretty soon the order was for 650 Soldiers to volunteer so I stepped forward and that started an avalanche. Pretty soon the Sergeant said that was enough. All the Soldiers who had volunteered were ordered to step forward. So again I led the way and after we were well separated from the Soldiers who remained behind we were ordered to halt. Then the Sergeant bellowed, "All youz guys go home; now the rest of youz guys, yer gonna police the post and there better not be a single butt on the ground after ya do it or yu'll hafta start all over and do it again."

Later, that day one of my friends said to me, "How did you have enough sense to volunteer?"

---

[32] Known to this day in the author's family as "the Army Comical Center."

"I can count just as well as the Sergeant."

26. The Bayonet Course

About the fifth week of basic training the boys were taken out to the bayonet course and shown how to fix a bayonet to their rifles. A pretend enemy Soldier was a gunnysack filled with straw with a face painted on the sack and the whole thing attached to a 4x4 wooden post, sunk into the ground and held in place by concrete. We were told to run up to the dummy, scream to distract the enemy for an instant, and then stab him as hard as we could with our bayonet. The Sergeant never told us to keep the bayonet horizontal so it would slip between the enemy's ribs, making it easier to kill him.

Like a dumb dodo, Fritz held his bayonet vertically and let out a mighty scream and jammed the bayonet ***all the way through*** the center of a new 4x4 post. He could not pull his bayonet out of the victim. One of the younger Sergeants whom Fritz rather liked came over to see what the trouble was. He asked, "What's wrong, Perfessor? Did we get carried away wid de program?"

When he tried to pull the rifle out of the post, he nearly ripped all the muscles out of his arm. So he called over another Sergeant, and both of them tried to extract the rifle from the 4x4. When they could not move it, one of them said, "Well Perfessor, it is your problem; don't come back to the barracks until you get the rifle out of that gdpq[33] post."

Fritz found that if he hung on the rifle, he could cause it to drop a few millimeters. Then, if he got under it and pushed up as hard as

---

[33] The key to decrypting **Bad Words** is explained in the footnote in the story "High School Chemistry."

possible, he could force it up a few millimeters. He rocked the rifle back and forth for several hours and eventually enlarged the hole enough that he could pull the bayonet out of the wood. But when he tried to walk, he simply fell over.

Eventually a Sergeant came to see what was wrong. He ordered Fritz to stand up and start marching. So Fritz stood up, and promptly fell on his face. This did not seem proper, so the Sergeant ordered Fritz to do it again. When Fritz fell over the second time the Sergeant fetched a Lieutenant. The Lieutenant ordered Fritz to stand up and start marching. He promptly fell on his face again. "What's wrong with you, Soldier?"

"I don't know, Sir, but every time I try to walk I just fall down."

"Does anything hurt?"

"No, Sir."

"Sergeant, get a meat wagon and take this here Soldier to the Hospital."

"Yes Sir, Lieutenant!"

At the Hospital, Fritz somehow got into an examining room and eventually a Full Colonel came in and asked what was wrong. When Fritz said he did not know but always fell over when he tried to walk, the Colonel told Fritz to sit on a chair while he whacked him below his knees with a rubber hammer. Nothing happened. He said, "That's funny."

"What is supposed to happen Colonel?"

"You're supposed to kick me when I hit you there."

"Well try it again, Sir."

He delivered a good stout whack and nothing happened. Then he said, "The reason you cannot walk is that your legs are not connected to the rest of your body. Does anything hurt?"

"No, Sir."

So with that, he had Fritz lie on an examining table, and as he looked straight into Fritz's eyes and started to lift his right leg, the stab of pain was excruciating.

"You felt that, didn't you?"

"Yes, Sir, how did you know, Sir?"

"Your eyes glazed over."

Then the Colonel told an Orderly who was standing nearby to put Fritz on a gurney, take him to the Orthopedic Ward and put him in the hardest empty bed you can find.

A week later Fritz went back to see the Colonel, who asked how he was. Fritz said he could walk to the bathroom without falling over.

"Do you think you can crawl across my floor?"

"Yes, Sir!"

"Then do it."

"Aye, aye, Sir."

"This is not the Navy, Soldier; did you forget that you are in the Army?

AFTER FRITZ CRAWLED ACROSS THE FLOOR, the Colonel ordered him to go back to the Orthopedic Ward, get back into bed, but on Monday, Wednesday and Friday afternoons he was to walk to the Base Library, sit at the desk for one hour and check out books, then walk back to the Ward and get back into bed and see the Doctor in two weeks. 40 years later Fritz learned that this was his Physical Therapy. Slowly, slowly, he got better, so that by December, he was able to go back on Active Duty and finish his basic training.

27. The Top Secret Army Chemical Center

Originally Fritz was assigned to become an Artillery Man and go to Fort Sill, Oklahoma to learn how to shoot the large field pieces with shells up to 115 mm in diameter. Fritz thought probably he would be chosen as a Spotter because his knowledge of Trigonometry would help land shots quickly on target. But you have to be able to lift enormous weights: Some of the shells were well over 150 pounds. Because he had hurt his back, he was ordered to never lift more than 25 pounds, and had to carry a paper at all times to show to any Officer who demanded that he lift more. So he was clearly not physically fit for the Artillery.

About the middle of December he was given a two-week leave and told to report to the U.S. Army Chemical Center on January 4th. But he had no idea where the Chemical Center was located. So it was off to see the First Sergeant who read the orders and said, "I cannot tell you where the Chemical Center is. It is a Top Secret Installation."

"But I have to know where it is, or how can I report there?"

"Go see the Captain."

The Captain repeated the story that he could not tell where the Chemical Center was because it was Top Secret.

"But Captain, I have to know because I do not want to be AWOL![34]"

"Good point, Soldier. Go down to Headquarters and ask for Major so and so."

After being passed through several hands, Fritz finally got to Major so and so (he can't even remember his name after all these years) who read his orders and said, "I can't tell you where it is. It is top secret. Go see the Colonel."

The Colonel was not about to tell, so Fritz asked him if it was on the East Coast or the West Coast, or somewhere in the middle like Utah?"

"Why do you want to know?"

"My parents live in Spokane and my Fiancée lives in Detroit. I certainly cannot afford to take a train trip twice across the country, so if I need to end up in Utah, I will go to Detroit first, and then go to Spokane

---

[34] Absent WithOut Leave

on my leave, but if the Chemical Center is in the East, then I will go to Spokane first, and then to Detroit.

"Oh! On January 3rd just go to the Baltimore, Maryland Bus Terminal and ask for a ticket to the Army Chemical Center."

"But Colonel Sir, do I have to ride the bus for a thousand miles?"

"No, it is not that far from Baltimore," but he still would not tell Fritz where this Top Secret Base was located!

28. Christmas

Fritz found a pay phone and telephoned Marion to tell her that he was going to Spokane first and then would come to Detroit. She was working as a Nurse at Bon Secours Hospital, about three blocks from her parents' home. She packed a suitcase, and asked her Dad to drop her off at the train station on his way to work next morning.

"Why? Where are you going?"

"I am going to Spokane."

Her Mom and Dad about passed out from shock, but she had been saving her pay checks and could easily afford the ticket. In the meantime, Fritz was trying to figure out how to get from Fort Bliss to Spokane. Somebody told him that if he could get to Albuquerque, New Mexico, he could fly by Apache Airlines to Boise, Idaho and at least he would be closer to home. But how to get to Albuquerque? **We need a car**!

Fritz called some car rental company, probably Hertz, but his RAM is failing rapidly and the memory is gone too. They told him the one-way price, so he collected money from five other guys who wanted to go to Albuquerque. They started an all-night drive, about 269 miles to the North. Remember, there were no Interstates in those days, just two lane U.S. highways.

The Soldiers got there in time for Fritz to catch his flight to Boise. The plane was a well-traveled DC3, which landed at many little air strips across New Mexico, Colorado, Wyoming, and Idaho. The Ticket Agent in Albuquerque should have kept Fritz off the airplane because his duffle bag was way overweight and he had all sorts of stainless steel Kitchen Utensils tied inside his Army Overcoat. He had gotten them cheaply in Juarez, Mexico, and thought they would be nice Christmas Presents for Marion. They are still in use after 58 years.

When the plane arrived in Boise, Fritz found a flight to Spokane, and phoned home. He got his Dad on the phone and asked him if he could pick him up at the Airport about 10:30 that night? Fritz's Mom did not hear the conversation, so Dad thought he would play a trick on her. At about 10 O'clock he said, "Alice, it is a beautiful moonlight night; why don't we go for a drive and see the Christmas lights? So he drove down the Monroe Street hill which is very steep, turned West on the highway to Cheney, and began the long climb out of the Spokane Valley to the Spokane Planes.

After a few miles he turned onto the road that led to the Airport, and Mom began to smell a rat!

"Why are we going to the Airport?"

"Don't know."

"Yes you do! Is Fritz coming tonight?"

"Guess we will have to see if he gets off the plane. Oh, by the way, we have to meet the Empire Builder[35] in two days at 11:30.

"So Marion is coming from Detroit too?"

It was a wonderful Christmas all around, and after a few days the Love Birds got on the Empire Builder and headed back East. About midnight on New Year's Eve, Marion opened her suitcase and produced a

---

[35] The train from Chicago through Spokane to the West Coast.

bottle of wine and some cheese and crackers and they had a little party right in their coach seats. Everything was going well until the train lurched a little and they spilled wine all over themselves. Marion does say she remembers that they smelled like drunken sailors for the rest of the trip. She got off the train in Detroit and went back to work, and in her spare time began addressing wedding invitations and doing everything you have to do to get ready for a wedding. Fritz took another train to Baltimore and somehow got a bus to Edgewood, Maryland and the gate to the Chemical Center.

When he finally arrived at the U.S. Army Chemical Center about midnight the day before he was supposed to report for duty, he told the Private, who was "Charge of Quarters" (COQ) for the night, about how no one would tell him where this Top Secret Base was located. The COQ started to laugh, and pulled out an Esso road map which showed a large area North of Baltimore and East of Highway 40, marked in big red letters, "**U.S. Army Chemical Center.**" Fritz has often wondered how many **Russian Spies** had trouble locating this Top Secret Base?

29. Eniwetok Atoll

His first assignment was to study Neutron Albedo, the non-specular reflection of neutrons from the ground. After all, we had to prepare the troops for a Nuclear War with Russia. The group he was in was also preparing equipment to take out to **ENIWETOK ATOLL**[36] in the South Pacific for a Hydrogen Bomb test. Several guys from his Lab went to the Pacific, but he stayed home; he had not been married very

---

[36] Google's definition of an atoll: "a ring-shaped reef, island, or chain of islands formed of coral."

long and a several month long separation from Marion did not seem like a fun thing to do.[37]

At the Atoll, and 15 miles from ground zero, two huge I-beams were sunk three meters deep into the coral and a large I-beam was welded between them, five meters above sea level. Our carefully prepared equipment was securely bolted to the horizontal I-beam, well above harm's way, or so we thought. But the blast was 17 Megatons instead of the 5 Megatons expected, and when the boys went to retrieve the equipment and the recorded data, there was no sign of the I-beams or of anything else. We never did find out whether they had melted in the blast, or simply been blown several kilometers to a **Far Distant Atoll**, or halfway there when they plunged several thousand fathoms to the **Bottom of the Ocean**. So much for several months' work!

30. A Shower of Rocks

Someone discovered that the Army Regulations (AR's) required one flag to be flown during daylight hours over each Army Base. But at the Army Chemical Center, we put up two flags each morning and took down two flags each evening: one at the Commanding General's Headquarters Building, and one at the Parade Ground. To the Lawyers who were Buck Privates this seemed like a clear violation of the AR's, and we should all be court-martialed and thrown into the brig[38] for such dereliction of duty. Not obeying the AR's is serious stuff!!!

Now every morning after the flag at the Parade Ground was up, and the Bugler had played whatever he was supposed to blow, a five inch

---

[37] The editor thinks this was the wrong choice. It's not every day you get to pioneer blowing up Hydrogen Bombs in the South Pacific.
[38] A brig refers to a prison, especially on a warship.

Howitzer was fitted with a blank shell and fired, awakening everybody, especially all the Officers who were sleeping in the Bachelor Office Quarters (BOQ) on the far side of the Parade Ground. One of the troops, who was often called upon to raise the flag, and was fairly tired of getting out of bed at 4 a.m., noticed that the Sergeant in charge of the flag detail did not bother to look up the barrel of the Howitzer before the charge was put in. This gave him an *Idea*, and a few days later someone stuffed a wadded up newspaper in the cannon and poured a bucket of gravel down the barrel on top of it. The next morning at 5 a.m., when the cannon was fired, all the windows in the BOQ dissolved in a shower of rocks.

The inspector General of the U.S. Army Chemical Corps came up to the Chemical Center from Washington D.C. to try to determine what had happened. Because I had spent several months in the Hospital at Fort Hood and was restricted in the weight I could lift (because of my bad back after getting carried away with my bayonet thrust), I never served on the Flag Raising Squad and they did not question me about the damage to the BOQ. I heard that the gravel was tested for fingerprints, but none were ever found, and, as far as I know, no one was ever charged in the disappearance of the windows.

31. Company B Drives Captain to the Korean War

The Captain of Company B was a little smarter than Sergeant Rock, but probably not much smarter. In 1957, when Valentine's Day rolled around, someone made a heart of a block of foam, covered it with a nice piece of aluminum foil and red velvet, stuck a bayonet in it and propped it up in the ward room where the Captain would be sure to see it when he came into the barracks first thing in the morning. The message accompanying the heart was **"MAY YOUR LIFE BE LONG, OH GLORIOUS[39] LEADER."**

The Captain ran into his office shouting for the First Sergeant to call Military Police (MP) and for the Duty Officer to send several men over immediately. This alerted several Privates who had Yeomen duty[40] that day, and one of them knew who had put up the heart. So that guy ran up the stairs into the barracks where the troops were still sleeping and got the culprit out of bed. He told him the Captain was furious and somebody was going to lose his dvv[41] over this.

It so happened that this particular Soldier worked in a Lab with about 100 monkeys, so he grabbed his pants and shirt and the heart, and drove as fast as he could to his Lab where he threw the offending valentine into the monkey cage. Naturally, the monkeys swarmed all over the valentine, covering it with hundreds of hand, finger and foot prints. Then the Soldier retrieved the heart and rushed back to the barracks, just beating the MP's, and propped it back in its original place on the balcony. Naturally the MP's could see that it had a lot of fingerprints, "Ah, this will be easy to identify the culprit who threatened the life of his Captain!"

The Army has complete sets of fingerprints of every Soldier because if he is killed in battle, perhaps the only way to identify the corpse is fingerprinting, but ahead of time, who knows which fingers will be available? The MP's had hundreds of fingerprints to inspect, and it took weeks, but they never found any match they could identify, and so no one was court-martialed. But the Captain had had enough of the disloyal troops he commanded at the Army Chemical Center and volunteered to lead an Infantry Company in Korea, not the safest assignment in the Army in 1957.

---

[39] The original of this document had "**GLORIUS**," which I assume is an inaccurate spelling of the actual message.
[40] The Yeomen did the typing and bookkeeping.
[41] The key to decrypting **Bad Words** is explained in the footnote in the story "High School Chemistry."

32. Ordering Plutonium

Because Fritz was then assigned the task of making a 50 curie neutron source that would have a half-life of at least 1000 years (so it would never have to be recalibrated), he started looking up half-lives of radioactive nuclei and finally settled on a Plutonium-Beryllium source using 50 kg of Plutonium. This seemed kind of extreme and he took his computations to Dr. Mahoney, who was in charge of this work. Eventually Mahoney decided to order the material, but it never came.

However, Fritz began to receive letters from Professors at Carleton saying the FBI had been all over campus asking questions about him; they even questioned his Dad about the work Fritz had done for him in his Accounting Practice while Fritz was in High School. Fritz could not figure out what was going on until he showed several letters to the other guys in his Lab. One of them said, "No wonder the FBI is on your tail; Mahoney ordered enough Plutonium to blow up the entire State of Maryland!"

Fritz had no idea what a critical mass was for an Atomic Bomb and had insufficient knowledge to calculate it. He doubts that Mahoney did either,[42] but he was in charge of the work, and he did have a Ph.D. in Physics. Fritz had only a BA! It seems likely that this is strong proof of the Theorem that Ph.D. stands for "Permanent Head Damage."

For revenge, someone wrote a limerick and posted it in the entrance to the Lab Building for all to see:

> There was an old fud[43] named Mahoney
> As a Physicist he was a phony
> As a liar and cheat

---

[42] Let's hope so.
[43] Old fud: An old and decrepit person.

He became Section Chief

And published Top Secret Baloney.

Fritz never did find out who the author was, but he learned that it was typed on the typewriter in the office of the Laboratory Director by someone wearing surgical gloves so as to leave no fingerprints, and then pinned to the bulletin board well after the Lab closed for the day. Fritz could not be told who the instigators were because he might **Crack under Extreme Questioning** (torture) and get the boys in serious trouble. Monkey paw prints could not be used in this case to cover the culprits' tracks because you must never repeat the same tactic twice, or eventually you will give away your secrets. The security guys are not stupid! Just not smart enough to outwit a bunch of drafted PFC's[44] with MS[45] and Ph.D. Degrees.

33. "How to Tell Time," by Sergeant Rock

Sergeant Rock was on the training team and he was assigned the task of teaching us how to tell time before we went out on the rifle range for our annual training in how to shoot the M-1 Rifle. Now Sergeant Rock might have been as smart as a rock, but we were all pretty skeptical. He was proud of the fact that he had graduated from 2nd grade and he "knowed a lot a stuff" that was valuable, and he "was gonna learn us how to tell time." Not a particularly good idea when the troops are all Scientists and Engineers, and all had at least a BS or a BA Degree and some had MS's and Ph.D.'s.

---

[44] Privates First Class.
[45] Master of Science.

So Sergeant Rock pointed to a huge target, the kind we used at 300 yards. Then he pointed to the upper right side **AND TOLD US VERY SOLEMNLY**[46], **THAT IF WE HIT THE TARGET THERE, IT WAS 2 O'CLOCK,** and the Soldier in the pit would telephone the guy who was monitoring our shooting and tell us so we could do better, because we had to hit the bull's-eye.

This went on for some time, and we learned about 8 O'clock, 11 O'clock and how many others I do not remember. Suddenly someone discovered that if all the troops who were sitting on the bleachers moved just a little bit together, the bleachers would fold up against the wall, and we would all fall in a heap on the floor. So that's what happened.

Sergeant Rock was dumbfounded and ordered the bleachers redeployed. We were told to sit on them again. As soon as he resumed his monologue the bleachers collapsed, and again we were all lying on top of each other on the floor. Then the Lieutenant Colonel, who was the highest ranking Officer present, swung into action and ordered the bleachers deployed again, but when he ordered us to sit down, the gdpq[47] things just collapsed a third time as though they had a mind of their own!

This was not to be tolerated! So he ordered us out onto the airfield to march for an hour or two until we learned how to behave ourselves and **SHOW SOME RESPECT FOR THE ARMY.** So there were about 800 Soldiers marching four abreast down the runway, and one of the Sergeants bellowed, **"COLUMN LEFT, MARCH!"**

And all khoo[48] broke loose. The left-most column did as they were ordered. The 2nd row marched straight ahead, the 3rd column did a

---

[46] **SOLUMELY** in the original.

[47] The key to decrypting **Bad Words** is explained in the footnote in the story "High School Chemistry."

[48] The key to decrypting **Bad Words** is explained in the footnote in the story "High School Chemistry."

snappy **TO THE REAR, MARCH!** And the 4th column did a **COLUMN RIGHT, MARCH!** Within seconds troops were all over the airfield.

It took quite a long time to get us back in proper formation. Then the Lt. Colonel, who was having apoplexy, stomped down the formation and asked me, "What command did you hear, Soldier?" I snapped him a salute and said "**TO THE REAR, MARCH, SIR.**" Then he asked a guy in the 4th column, "What command did you hear, Soldier?" "**COLUMN RIGHT, MARCH, SIR.**"

After checking out a dozen Soldiers we started off marching again and this time the command "**WAS COLUMN RIGHT, MARCH!**" Again there was instant chaos as the four columns went left, straight ahead, to the rear, and right. The poor Colonel tried a third time and then gave up. Clearly we were all hard of hearing, and not very loyal Soldiers. So ended the training for that Saturday.

34. PHELPS JOINS THE TRAINING TEAM

I do not remember exactly how it came about that I was placed on the training team. I found myself talking to the Lt. Colonel about teaching the boys how to read maps. I had to prepare a detailed report of what I would do, and have the Colonel approve it before I could implement the plan. So I worked up a brilliant lecture on *conformal mapping*, which you can read about in any advanced calculus book.

The idea IS **VERY SIMPLE**. We want to map[49] the surface of the earth onto a plane. So we set the earth in the middle of a huge sheet

---

[49] This means to define a function which takes any given point on the surface of the earth (assumed to be a sphere), and sends it to some point on the entire infinite two

of paper with the South Pole at the origin of a Cartesian (X, Y) coordinate system. We rotate the globe so that Greenwich, England is directly above the positive X axis. This establishes the Prime Meridian.

In order to define to where a point p on the surface of the earth maps, we start at the North Pole and we draw the unique straight line through the interior of the earth which hits the point p and extend the line until it hits the X-Y plane. The intersection is the point to which p maps. The North Pole itself maps to a nice point we add to the set of points in the plane and call "infinity." This turns out to be a technically proper[50] or *conformal* mapping of points on the sphere of the earth's surface to points on the plane (augmented with "infinity", the image of the North Pole), and this ***conformal map*** is very useful for some obscure purposes.

I did about three long days of mathematical manipulations to finally develop the equations that would allow me to calculate the X and Y coordinates of the image of any point on the surface of the earth whose latitude was φ and whose longitude was θ. After these equations were developed, I had to work out the inverse equations, and again it took most of a week of intensive work to get it all figured out. Then it was back to the Colonel's office with everything written up for his approval.

I decided to include some tricks I had learned about how the Germans make military maps using a Stoss Line (thrust line) and measuring angles from the Stoss Line rather than giving azimuth compass directions. This makes it impossible for an enemy to intercept a message and know what it means, but it is perfectly clear to the receiving Soldiers, **IF** they have the Stoss Line already plotted on their map ahead of time.

---

dimensional X-Y plane. The editor has taken the liberty to add some mathematical precision to the discussion at several points.

[50] A bijective (one to one and onto), angle preserving map from the earth's surface to $R^2 \cup \infty$.

Now remember that most of our Saturday training sessions were similar to Sergeant Rock's teaching us how to tell time: boring as khoo.[51] And quite a few of the Soldiers had Ph.D.'s in Science or Mathematics or Engineering. So after I delivered a two hour lecture on *conformal mapping* covering several blackboards with equations and diagrams, the Soldiers leaped to their feet and cheered and clapped and yelled and shouted. They would not stop until Sergeant Rock got up and told 'em to "**SHUT UP!**" He started to chew out their dvvhv[52] for being disrespectful of me because, while he didn't understand what I had done, it must be O.K. because the Colonel approved it. That just started the clapping and yelling all over again. And it went on and on.

The next Monday the Colonel sent someone to the Lab to fetch me, and when I got to his office he said he was going to court-martial[53] me for insulting the Army! Why? "Because the troops rioted after the training session on Saturday." I pointed out that **HE HAD APPROVED** my lesson plan, including all the Math I did on the blackboards, whereupon he called in Sergeant Yakabonus, First Sergeant of Company B (my company).

He asked Sergeant Yakabonus if he had attended the Saturday training. Yup, he was there. Then he asked if the troops rioted after I finished. The Sergeant thought for a while and said there was a lot of shouting and clapping and cheering, but he did not think it was a riot. Then the Colonel asked Sergent Yakabonus if I had insulted the Army. Sergeant Yakabonus thought and thought and then said, "I didn't

---

[51] The key to decrypting **Bad Words** is explained in the footnote in the story "High School Chemistry."
[52] The key to decrypting **Bad Words** is explained in the footnote in the story "High School Chemistry."
[53] Of course this is spelled "court marshal" in the original.

understand much about what this here Soldier was talking about, but if anybody was insulted it was his own i-lqj[54] fault."

After the Colonel's eyes popped back into his head, he realized his Chief Witness could not be relied upon to lie at my court-martial. He informed me I was no longer on the training team, and kicked me out of his office. So I dodged a bullet, or perhaps a 225 mm artillery shell.

There must have been two dozen Soldiers that told me, "Your Lecture was the first decent training session I have attended since I arrived at the Army Chemical Center." But my brilliance was doomed to the grave after that Saturday morning training session. Indeed I had anticipated that result as I worked up my lecture. Oh well, such is life in the U.S. Army. I never could understand why the Americans won WWII: The Germans were a lot smarter.

35. THE RIFLE RANGE OR "LEARNING HOW TO SHOOT"

Some weeks after Sergeant Rock had taught us how to tell time, we were ordered to hike from the Saturday training theater to the storage room where we were told to pick up our assigned rifle. Then we were marched to the rifle range which was a pretty long way off. Naturally we thought that a decent **ARMY** would haul us the several miles in buses, but the Lt. Colonel must have thought that we deserved to walk because of the chaos we had caused on the airfield.

The firing line was about fifty meters of sand, long enough for fifty Soldiers to fire at one time, each with a Sergeant beside him so as to

---

[54] Presumably a word used much less frequently in such situations in the 1950s than today. The key to decrypting **Bad Words** is explained in the footnote in the story "High School Chemistry."

make sure we did not shoot any of our fellow grunts. There were targets at different distances: 100, 200 and 300 yards.

The targets were huge sheets of paper with a large black circle in the center, surrounded by concentric circles of black with uncolored annuli between the circles. The targets were numbered 5 points for the bull's-eye, and the annuli were numbered 4, 3, 2, 1. The targets were mounted on a frame made of 2x4's which could be pushed above the pit where the Soldiers were well protected from being shot by being in a trench about 2.5 meters below the flying bullets.

As luck would have it, we were carefully instructed on which target to shoot at by Sergeant Rock, who was not much smarter than the last time. He was very careful to tell us we **MUST SHOOT EXACTLY AT THE TARGET HE WAS POINTING TO.** After five shots the targets would be pulled down, and each Soldier's score would be reported to the Sergeant lying next to him on the firing line. The Sergeant would communicate with the pit on a field telephone.

Naturally we misunderstood Sergeant Rock and thought that *we all* had to shoot at the central target he was pointing to. And so, when we were ordered to load and lock one round of armor-piercing ammunition and then to commence firing, it happened (just by accident), that **every** Soldier fired at the 2x4 supports on the two sides of the middle target, and so the target crashed into the pit!

This was the target Sergeant Rock was using when he had told us we must obey orders and shoot exactly where he told us to shoot. We certainly did not want to disobey orders! When the supports were completely shattered by 50 bullets, naturally there was khoo[55] to pay, and we were all ordered to stand at attention while the Lt. Colonel stomped

---

[55] The key to decrypting **Bad Words** is explained in the footnote in the story "High School Chemistry."

up and down the line and demanded to know why we had fired at the wrong target. I said Sergeant Rock had told us to fire at the target he was pointing to or he would eat our dvvhv[56] for lunch, and we certainly did not want to provide Sergeant Rock with his mid-day meal for not doing exactly as ordered.

Eventually we had to resume shooting and we behaved ourselves fairly well. But the Company Captain called me into his office the next Monday morning and told me he was going to court-martial my dvv[57] for cheating on the rifle range! I asked him what was wrong, and he said I had shot a score of 50 with 10 shots in the bull's-eye, and nobody could shoot that well, so clearly I had cheated!

I asked him who had scored my target because I could not do it myself, seeing as how I was 300 yards from the pit. So he looked at the signed score sheet. It had been signed by Sergeant Yakabonus, the First Sergeant of Company B. So the Captain let out a bellow for Sergeant Yakabonus to come into his office and verify that it was his signature on the target report.

"YES SIR, DATS MY SIGNATURE, SIR!"

"Well Sergeant, why did you lie about the score this here Soldier got?"

"Captain **SIR**, the guy pulling target in the pit reported the score to me and I just wrote it down like I am supposed to, **SIR**. He said there were 10 holes in the black, **SIR;** I ain't never seen such good shooting, **SIR!!**"

So then it was my turn. "Soldier, how do you account for this score?"

---

[56] The key to decrypting **Bad Words** is explained in the footnote in the story "High School Chemistry."

[57] The key to decrypting **Bad Words** is explained in the footnote in the story "High School Chemistry."

"Well Sir, I think I must have a brand new rifle because I can't seem to miss if I take time to sight properly!" The next thing I knew I was called out at a Saturday training formation and given a **SHARPSHOOTER MEDAL**! Which I still have.

36. One Way to Get Discharged From the Army

I was drafted in June of 1956 and entered the Army in July for two years of active duty. Upon receipt of the President's letter I immediately wrote Professor Dennison, Chairman of Physics at the University of Michigan, that I would be unable to serve as a Teaching Fellow in the fall of 1956, but would return to Michigan to complete my MS Degree in the fall of 1958.

In the spring of 1958, someone told me that he had been studying the AR's, and that any Soldier could apply for discharge up to six weeks early to attend College, so I wrote Professor Dennison and told him I would apply for early discharge in case there was any chance that I could resume my Teaching Fellowship for the summer session of 1958.

The response was immediate; he would be happy to have me back and had assigned me to teach four sections of Lab with 20 Students per section. Now it was a matter of filing the proper papers with the Army Chemical Corps. So we went to work and tried to do everything correctly, but soon after submitting the paperwork, the Army denied my request for discharge five weeks early!

Now what do we do? Marion telephoned Bill Baker, one of the Ministers that had married us in March of my first year of active duty. Bill was Campus Minister at First Presbyterian Church in Ann Arbor. Bill went to see Ralph Sawyer, Dean of the Horace H. Rackham School of Graduate Studies and Professor of Physics. Bill was armed with a copy of my request for early discharge and the appropriate passage from the AR's permitting it.

Dean Sawyer wrote a very nice letter to the Commanding General of the U.S. Army Chemical Corps to the effect that, based upon the published AR's, the University of Michigan had granted me an Assistantship, and that the University was expecting me to teach 80 Students, as stated in my application. Clearly it was not easy to find candidates able to teach courses such as Physics Laboratories because to do so required a BS in Physics as preparation, and such people were not walking around campus by the thousands. To find a replacement for me would be extremely difficult, and would severely impact the University's efforts to provide quality education for the Students who were expecting to enroll in my assigned classes. Dean Sawyer concluded his letter by asking the Commanding General to reconsider the rejection of my request.

Dean Sawyer's letter was mailed to the Commanding General of the U.S. Army Chemical Corps, in care of Private Phelps, U.S. Army Chemical Center, Edgewood, Maryland. Once the letter was in my hands, I did not know what to do, so I went to see Sergeant Yakabonus. He sent me to the Captain, who immediately sent me to Headquarters to talk to the Duty Sergeant in General Gurnsey's office. The Duty Sergeant read the letter and said, "I am not going to touch dis wif a ten foot pole; dis is going straight to General Gurnsey."

Minutes later General Gurnsey ordered me to take the letter immediately to Washington D.C., to the Headquarters of the U.S. Army Chemical Corps at Gravelly Point, and I was given a pass to leave the Base for as long as necessary to carry out my orders. Somehow, I cannot remember how, I found out that Gravelly Point was at the Washington National Airport and was told how to find the appropriate gate. Then I called Marion, who immediately started to brew a pot of extra thick starch to stiffen up my best uniform, and, as soon as my pants had a crease that would cut a sheet of paper, we left for Washington D.C., a fairly short drive South on Highway 40 from the Chemical Center.

We found the appropriate gate, and, just as expected, it was guarded by a Soldier with a rifle on his shoulder. I saluted the Guard, walked through the gate and started to look around. A dozen or so Very High Ranking Officers were walking towards me so I had to stiffen to attention and snap them my best salute. All the Officers disappeared through a doorway, but a Full Colonel hung back and asked, "Who are you looking for Soldier?"

"Just the Commanding General of the Army Chemical Corps, Sir. I have a letter for him."

The Colonel said, "Let me have the letter. I'll see that he gets it."

"Yes, Sir," and I gave him the letter.

He told me to follow him into his office where he sat behind a huge desk, opened the letter and read it through thoughtfully. He said, "This does not need to go to the Commanding General; I can handle this myself." With that he pulled out a form, filled in a few blanks, signed it, and said, "Take this back to the Chemical Center and give it to General Gurnsey's First Sergeant. And by the way, congratulations on the resumption of your studies at the University of Michigan."

I was so shell-shocked I cannot remember if he told me, "**GO BLUE!**" because he was a Michigan Man himself, but he might have been. A couple days later I was ordered to Fort Dix to undergo the proper discharge procedures. Marion started to pack up all of our stuff. A few days later I rented a U-Haul trailer and we started the journey to Grosse Pointe Park, to Marion's parents' home.

That proved to be an exciting adventure because, while Marion was driving, we blew out a tire on the trailer in a tunnel on the Pennsylvania Turnpike. We drove half a mile or more on a flat tire because we had to get out of the tunnel to let other cars pass: The road in the tunnel was only two lanes with no shoulder or pull outs.

And so ended my two years of active duty in the U.S. Army. In recent years I have been called upon to stand and be recognized for my military service. It is very hard to do that and have dry eyes when it is over.

Part VII. Back to Graduate School (1958-1964)

37. Closed Doors and on to Kalamazoo College

It was good to get back to Graduate School and spend my time doing something creative. I finished my MS during the summer session of 1958, and thought I would be able to start on my Ph.D. in the fall, but that was not to be. I interviewed a lot of Professors about possible thesis topics and decided that I would work for a young Professor, whose name I can no longer remember. He was interested in making the strongest magnetic field that had ever been created, and had accumulated a huge number of very large, very high voltage capacitors (their old name was "condensers"), which we would charge in parallel and then discharge in series. After I had decided to work for this guy, I tried all day to find him to tell him I wanted to be his Ph.D. Student, but he was never in his office.

Eventually I went home for dinner and Marion said, "Some young guy in the Department dropped dead today; he was jumping on a trampoline at the gym. He got off, sat on the floor and said 'I am getting too old for this jumping stuff,' and then keeled over, dead.

Yup, that is why I could never find him in his office. Some years later I learned that his Daughter finished her Ph.D. in Physics in the Department, but I do not remember whether she tried to build a four Tesla magnetic field or did a thesis on some other topic.

I was somewhat bummed by this turn of events and went to see Professor Dennison. He informed me that he would not have let me form a thesis committee anyway because I was not getting all As.

I said, "Professor Dennison, there are 73 Students in your Theoretical Mechanics class; 70 of us are Theorists and 3 of us are Experimentalists and I cannot push a pencil fast enough to compete with a Theorist on his own turf. Why don't you select the best Theorist in your class and take him down to the basement and see if he can hook a voltmeter into a circuit properly."

Professor Dennison replied, "Are you crazy? He would blow up the voltmeter."

So I said, "Well, who is the better Physicist, someone who can only think about a problem, or someone who can actually do some Physics?"

He did not answer but repeated, "In any case you may not form a thesis committee until you get all As in your courses." That was never going to happen, so I left his office feeling quite discouraged.

The Bendix Company was looking for Engineers and would consider Physics Students if they had to, so I decided to apply, and at the end of the fall semester I was offered a job starting in January. I was not too happy about this.

A few days later, Mrs. Barrons, the Department Secretary, stopped me in the hall and said, "The Dean of Kalamazoo College is desperate for some help. Would you be interested in teaching for him starting in January?"

"YES!"

"Call Dean Barrett at this number; I think Professor Dennison recommended you to Dr. Barrett."

I telephoned and Dean Barrett asked me to come for an interview. I had classes six days a week, so Sunday was the only possibility.

It was an interesting interview, but I do not think it was going particularly well until the Dean asked me why I wanted to be a College Professor.

I said, "Professor Butler at Carleton is not the smartest Physicist I have ever studied under, but he gives us everything he has. I want to be like him."

The turnaround was instantaneous. "I will pay you $6,500.00 if you will teach both Physics and Math for me spring semester, and you can rent a College house in Faculty Row for the semester." It may have taken a whole millisecond for me to accept the job! I could not think fast enough to decide in a microsecond or less.

As soon as final exams ended in Ann Arbor, I got a pile of boxes and we started to pack up for our move to Kalamazoo, and, oh yes, I had to resign from Bendix before I started. We moved on a day of a serious ice storm and slid all the way to Kalamazoo, but Marion did a good job, and we did not crash into anything. But we could hardly get the car and trailer up the hill to our new home: It was so slippery.

38. Teaching at Kalamazoo

I started my teaching with a junior course in Classical Mechanics and two Math courses, College Algebra and Trigonometry. One day during an Algebra exam, I noticed a guy hanging half-way across the aisle, looking at the paper of one of the smarter girls in the class. I walked down to see what was going on, and, when he eventually looked up, I put an appropriate grade on his exam, pointed at the door, and told him to get out and that I would see him in the Dean's Office after class.

Kalamazoo College had an extensive evaluation form for the Students to fill out at the end of the term. One question was, "Would you recommend this Professor to a friend?" I will never forget the answer of one of my girls: "**YES**, but I'd sure warn 'em first." I took that as a complement, but perhaps it was meant as an insult. I never did ask what she meant, but I still have her evaluation!

Dean Barrett told me I could stay on the faculty at K College forever, but I would have to get a Ph.D. someplace and so he suggested I go to Moo U[58] or Notre Dame. I told him I would not do a Ph.D. part time but would leave and finish it up as fast as possible.

"That is fine, but I will not hold a job for you while you are gone."

"O.K., and if you do not want me back when I finish my Ph.D., I will just find a faculty position elsewhere."

39. Planning for a Ph.D.

So I began to think about possible thesis topics and where I could do my Ph.D. I decided that I would like to be a Spectroscopist and I found three possibilities: Purdue University, MIT or the University of Alberta. Hum, Purdue is a Big Ten University just like Michigan, and if I can't get through Michigan I probably cannot get through Purdue either, and I sure am not a good enough Physicist to get through MIT, **those guys are GOOD**. That left Alberta. When I found that Professor Newbound, the Dean of Science, was a graduate of Dean Harrison's Spectroscopy Lab at MIT, I thought I might possibly have found the golden grail!

In August I wrote a letter to Professor Newbound asking him if he would chair a thesis committee for me if I moved to Edmonton and enrolled in the University of Alberta. I sent transcripts, and faculty at Carleton, Michigan and Kalamazoo wrote letters of recommendation. In early September I had an answer: He would be delighted to have me come up North, and he would offer me a position as Sessional Instructor at CAD $2500.00[59] per year until I finished my studies.

---

[58] Michigan State University.

$2500.00/year? Something seemed wrong. Dennison only paid me $1620/year at Michigan to be a Teaching Fellow! So I made arrangements to visit Professor Dennison and asked him what was wrong with the offer. It just seemed like too much money. Professor Denison read the letter carefully and then said, "I wish our Fellowships were that big. Alberta has recently struck **OIL** and they're trying to build a **World Class University**. They are putting a lot of resources into it. This is a very fine offer; you would be extremely foolish to turn it down!"

That settled it. I held Professor Dennison in very high esteem; that is why I asked his advice. How could I not take it? I wrote Professor Newbound to tell him I would accept his offer provided he would let me start in the fall of 1960 because I had promised to teach at Kalamazoo College for 1959-1960.

His response was instantaneous, "Yes, come in September 1960, I will have a Fellowship for you." So I stayed on for the year at Kalamazoo, which gave them a year to hire a replacement for me.

40. FINDING A MATHEMATICIAN FOR KALAMAZOO: JEAN CALLOWAY

When I told Dean Barrett I was going to Alberta, he lamented the fact that he had not been able to find a new Head for the Math Department. I said, "Why don't you hire away the best man at Carleton?"

"I would if I knew who he was."

"I can tell you; it's Jean Calloway."

So the Dean wrote Jean, but there was no response, and he was, of course, a little miffed. In the fall Jean wrote him and apologized for not

---

[59] The Canadian dollar was worth about US $1.03 in 1960.

answering sooner, but he had been on Sabbatical leave at Princeton, at the Institute for Advanced Studies. The Dean's letter had been inadvertently thrown in the box of mail for him to read when he returned to Northfield and was not forwarded to him as it should have been. But if the position was still open, he was interested.

When the Dean told me, I said, "Do you know that Professor Calloway's Wife also has a Ph.D. in Mathematics, so if you need an extra Mathematician you will have a ready source of help on campus?" Professor Calloway came to Kalamazoo just as I was leaving for Alberta. I was very sorry to miss teaching for Jean: I am sure I would have learned a lot.

When Fred[60] was ready to go to College, he chose Kalamazoo. It was clear that he would be a Math major and I really wanted him to study with Professor Calloway, but their schedules never meshed, and Fred graduated from K without ever having Jean for a Teacher. I have always been sad about that: Jean was as good as they come!

41. THE MOVE TO EDMONTON (1960)

We needed a trailer for our move to Edmonton. Renting a U-Haul would cost way too much money, so the alternative was to build my own. I found a Manufacturer who would make the running gear, four wheels and a frame of 2 inch heavy walled pipe. I hired someone to build a trailer hitch for my Plymouth and weld it in place. Then all I had to do was to buy a lot of lumber and build a huge box about 4 meters long by 3 meters wide by 2 meters high.

---

[60] The reference is to Fritz's hitherto unmentioned firstborn Son Fred IV.

Fred IV had come to live with us in January of 1960, so I would take him outside while the construction was going on and explain to him what I was doing: Using U bolts to connect the wood to the pipe frame or whatever the job was for that day. He seemed to enjoy it and it gave Mφm[61] a little time off from her job as Perpetual Babysitter.

Marion's Dad came home one day with a bolt of Naugahyde[62] and Marion sewed it into a trailer cover. When she was finished, I added many large grommets along the edges so it could be tied down with 6.35 mm manila hemp to keep the contents of the trailer dry, just in case it happened to rain on our way to Edmonton.

As we were passing through Detroit, the trailer fishtailed and dropped table legs on Woodward Avenue. We returned to Grosse Pointe Park, reloaded the trailer with more weight on the trailer hitch instead of on the wheels, said goodbye again, and then resumed our journey.

Otherwise, the trip to Edmonton was fairly uneventful until I was rolling through Alberta at close to 83 km/hr on new pavement which suddenly ended. We flew off the edge and dropped about 7.5 cm to the old road. The jar of smashing onto the old pavement was enough to cause a wheel to crack and the tire to instantly lose all its air. Rolling a few meters on that flat tire destroyed what had been a new tire a few minutes earlier. At the tire shop (I suppose I should spell that "tyre" like the Canadians do) they had a Plymouth for a parts car, and readily sold me a new wheel and tyre to go on it, and we continued on our journey.

---

[61] Marion has become known as "Momster" (a term of endearment not used in this document), and also as "Em-Zero-Em," in this outlier of a family. The author has spelled the latter "Mφm" because, "it's hard to tell a zero from an o." So the Greek letter phi in this word stands for a zero.

[62] From Wikipedia: Naugahyde is an American brand of artificial leather.

42. The Northern Lights

We camped along the way, and one evening, in a city campground in Calgary, we had a fantastic display of the Aurora Borealis.[63] Intense bands of shimmering green light (from a forbidden transition in the Oxygen Spectrum) started at any point on the Horizon and shot to the Zenith. It was the most fantastic Aurora I have ever seen.

I did not put up the tent that night. It was clear and there was no hint of rain. Fred, who was nine months old, was bundled up in his snowsuit to keep warm, lying on his back between Mφm and Dad, watching the sky. He had Mφm's heavy wool Michigan M blanket pulled up to his chin to provide extra warmth.

I thought it was a good time for a lesson on Atomic Emission Spectroscopy, so we talked about Oxygen atoms and how an electron could jump from a higher energy level to a lower energy level, and, in the process, emit a green photon. But the green emission line is a "forbidden transition," meaning, in this case, there had to be an additional collision between the excited Oxygen atom and another Oxygen atom in order to conserve L, the Angular Momentum Quantum Number.

Fred seemed to be taking it all in and thinking about it. This I interpreted as an indication that he might become a Physicist someday. Eventually he had a double major, Physics and Mathematics, at Kalamazoo College and went on to receive a Ph.D. from the University of Utah. Altogether, it was a very satisfying conversation with my Son, even if he did not contribute much to the conversation.

---

[63] The Northern Lights.

43. Professor Newbound

K. B. Newbound was raised in Winnipeg and graduated from the University of Manitoba. His education was interrupted by World War II when he worked for the Canadian Navy devising sound generating gear to attract German Acoustic Torpedoes, which were designed to seek out the loudest sound made by a ship (the propeller), and blow the ship to bits. After the war, Professor Newbound earned his Ph.D. in Physics with George Harrison, Dean of Science at the Massachusetts Institute of Technology.

Professor Newbound was a most remarkable and kind person. I was truly blessed to be his Graduate Student. There were numerous instances when he saved my neck and didn't even know it.

For example, Professor Manchester, who ran the Low Temperature Lab across the hall from the Spectroscopy Lab, thought I should fetch him his tea twice a day. I told him I would be happy to fetch his tea assuming that **THE DEAN OF THE FACULTY OF SCIENCE**[64] told me that was part of my duties.

"No, no, no! Don't ask the **DEAN**; I shall fetch my own tea."

Actually, I would have been happy to do that for Manchester because his Technicians taught me many valuable lessons such as how to sweat copper pipe fittings together using solder containing at least 50% tin. I have used what they taught me many times during the past half-century, including for all the plumbing for the house I built in Mount Pleasant.

---

[64] i.e., Newbound.

44. Candidacy Exam

Professor Newbound came to the Lab one day and told me that the Department was going to switch from oral candidacy exams to written exams. I told him one reason I had come to Alberta was the oral candidacy exam because I cannot compete with a good Theorist at his own game, and four-hour exams in Mechanics, Electricity and Magnetism, Optics and Quantum Mechanics would be killers. His instantaneous response was, "You shall have an oral candidacy exam; I shall tell Hugh (Grayson-Smith, the Head of the Physics Department)." Deans have a lot of power when it comes to Department Heads, and can tell them what will or will not happen.

A natural question is why would I prefer an oral exam to a written exam. I can solve tough Physics questions, but often it will take me a day to figure out how to ask the right question or where to start attacking a given situation and then a second day to carry out the solution. I am able to do the tough Math, but not easily. I have to work very deliberately and with extreme care. I know a lot of Physicists and Physics Students who can push a ball point pen much faster than I can, and I just felt that I could display my knowledge of Physics in an oral exam and avoid proving that Theoretical Physics should be left to Theorists.

When I took Quantum Mechanics for the third time, Professor Schiff said, "Phelps, you spend all your time trying to prove the obvious."

I could only respond with, "It may be obvious to you Professor Schiff, but I have to convince myself that the jump you want me to make is actually correct Physics." I love to do experimental work because I think I am pretty good at it. Theoretical Physics is hard work for me because I simply lack the ability to think like a Theorist.

I can make this clear by giving a question that Professor Betts asked me my on my candidacy exam:

Consider a cube with a 1 Ohm resistor along each edge. Then take any vertex and go to the diagonally opposite vertex and calculate the resistance of the network.

So I drew a cube on the board and thought to myself, "I can solve this problem with Kirchhoff's Laws; I will only have to solve 12 equations in 12 unknowns." And so I drew 12 currents labeled I_1 through I_{12}, and 12 resistors all labeled R, and started writing down the loop and junction equations.

Professor Betts was getting a little agitated and eventually he almost leaped out of his seat and shouted, "**No, Phelps! Think!**"

I answered, "Professor Betts, I am sure you have a very clever way to solve this problem and I do not know what that is, but I know Kirchhoff's Laws are correct Physics. It may be **Stupid Physics**, but it is **Correct Physics**. If you will just sit there patiently, I shall solve this problem for you, and I hope to have your solution by next May. I have to solve only 12 equations in 12 unknowns. That will take a bit of work, about $12!$[65] operations, or about 150 million steps, but I can do it correctly." Then I looked at Professor Newbound who was laughing uproariously, and I knew I had tangled with a Theorist and won.

Eventually the Examining Committee dismissed me while they considered whether I knew enough Physics to be allowed to proceed to my thesis. Later that afternoon Professor Newbound came to the Lab and said, "Well, you passed unanimously, but the Examining Committee recommends that you do an experimental thesis. I assured them that that is exactly what you intend to do."

I have often wondered how many members of the Committee would have voted to throw me out if I had **NOT BEEN** a Student of the

---

[65] In Mathematics $12!$ means $12 \times 11 \times \ldots \times 2 \times 1$ which is actually closer to 490 million than 150 million.

Dean of Science. I think I have an inkling because, after I had passed my thesis exam, the Department faculty discussed whether I should be offered a tenure track faculty position. Professor Manchester said I was a "meathead" and other things that were less flattering. Finally Professor Grayson-Smith told Manchester that he had heard enough and he thought it was time to ask Dean Newbound for his opinion.

The Dean said, "Well, Dr. Phelps has a deaf Daughter,[66] and there is no suitable School in Edmonton for her. Besides, why would he stay at Alberta at CAD $6,000/year[67] when the University of Michigan has offered him a job at $11,000/year?" Professor Newbound told me, when Manchester's Mandible hit the floor, it was the most satisfying deflation of a pompous windbag he had ever witnessed!!!

45. Learning to Write Computer Programs

My thesis was to determine Class A Standards[68] of wavelength for atoms of ^{198}Mercury and ^{86}Krypton. Shortly after my thesis was completed, the International Committee of Weights and Measures adopted the Orange Emission Line of ^{86}Krypton as the world standard of length. I was trying to measure wavelengths of light waves to an accuracy of at least eight significant figures (1 part in 50 million), but occasionally I got lucky and achieved 1 part in 500 million.

I had to make thousands of mathematical computations and I used two Rotary Marchant Calculators,[69] bolted side by side to my Lab

---

[66] Dorothy, born in 1962.
[67] At this time the Canadian dollar was worth around 93 US cents.
[68] Class A means "extremely precise," and although I could not find the precise definition, it is something like one part in 50 million.
[69] In the original the author has "Rotary Merchant Calculators." As for the calculators

table so that I could use one machine with my left hand, and one machine with my right hand. It took me about 15 minutes to make one of the needed computations, assuming of course that I made no mistakes requiring me to start over.

Then one day Professor Newbound came to the Lab and said, "We have just received a new IBM 1620 Card Program Calculator and Professor Harold is in charge of the computer. I wonder if you could use it to speed up your computations? Professor Harold was one of the Physicists on my Thesis Committee. After Professor Newbound left the Lab, I decided to take the Elevator to the 6th floor and have a little talk with Professor Harold. I asked him to teach me how to write computer programs and input data.

He said he was using mostly FORTRAN and he taught me how to use nested parentheses to write very complicated equations in one line of code. The rules are pretty simple: If S stands for the sum of two numbers and A and B are the two numbers you want added, you write $S = A+B$, and if D is their difference you write $D = A-B$. Similarly, if P is their product, then $P = A*B$, and if Q is their quotient, then $Q = A/B$.

After my lesson in Computer Programming, I went back to the basement and wrote a program to calculate what I needed. I typed up 100 cards using data I had calculated by hand, and therefore, for which I knew the answers, went back to the 6th floor and said to Professor Harold, "Here is my program; here is my data. How soon can I get the results?"

He looked at me somewhat surprised and said, "You must debug the program first." I didn't know what "debug" meant. So I asked him, and he said you have to correct all the errors you typed into the program.

"Why would I want to put errors into the program? Unless you told me a lie, there are no errors in that program. It will work."

---

themselves, see Wikipedia.

He thought he would show me up, and so took me over to the computer, put my program in the card reader and pushed a button. The computer ate the deck and after a few seconds began to punch out another deck of cards.

"Humm. That's funny; that is not supposed to happen."

"What is this deck of cards for?"

"The computer converted your source program to machine language that it can understand."

Then he took the machine language program, put it back in the card reader, pushed the start button again and soon a third deck of cards appeared. "That's really funny." He took the deck of cards to another machine which he called a "line printer," and it printed out the data which I read, checking off each result, and saying helpful things like, "that's correct, that's correct, that's correct."

So the computer was calculating correctly what I wanted it to. Each computation took 2.3 seconds instead of 15 minutes. Wow, that really speeded up my work: Now it took 230 seconds instead of 25 hours to do 100 computations. I returned to my Lab with the deck of cards and the printed data.

It was not long before Professor Newbound appeared in the Lab and asked, "What did you just do to Professor Harold? He just came to my office muttering about some fantastic program you wrote."

I explained to Professor Newbound that I did not know what "debug" meant, or much else about the IBM 1620 computer for that matter, but it computed in 2.3 seconds what it took me 15 minutes to do by hand. The Dean left the Lab shaking his head and saying, "I think I shall go have a little further talk with Professor Harold."

The IBM 1620 probably saved me a year of computation time on my thesis, and it was always a fun day when I could shock a Professor, and especially the Dean of Science.

46. Professor L. E. H. Trainer (1962)

One morning in the fall of 1962 I was working in the Spectroscopy Lab. I was grinding the two ends of the spacers for the Fabry-Perot Etalons[70] that Nick Riebeck made for me in the Department machine shop. The end planes had to be parallel to within a fraction of a wavelength of light. Professor L. E. H. Trainer, an incredibly good Theoretical Physicist, had been assigned to teach the Advanced Optics Laboratory. I have never understood **WHY** Hugh Grayson-Smith assigned a Theorist to teach a Lab class. Had the Head of the Physics Department forgotten that there is a difference between Experimentalists and Theorists? In any case, I have always suspected that Professor Trainer was one of the Theorists who attended my candidacy examination who recommended to the Dean that I be required to do an experimental thesis.

As I recall (but my memory is not as good as it was 61 years ago), it was nearly noon when I heard the door to the Lab open. When I looked up, I was surprised to see Professor Trainer invading my sanctum sanctorum.[71] I asked him if I could help and he said he needed the Dean's help. I said I thought Dean Newbound was in The Deanery and asked him what was wrong, because something was obviously troubling him.

"I have been trying since early this morning to find some gdpq[72] interference fringes in a Michelson Interferometer I need this afternoon for the Optics Lab I am teaching. I cannot find any circular fringes at all."

---

[70] Try Wikipedia
[71] Latin for the Biblical "Holy of Holies."
[72] The key to decrypting **Bad Words** is explained in the footnote in the story "High School Chemistry."

"Well Professor Trainer, I may be able to help you; would you like to try me to try to find the rings for you? That way we will not have to bother the Dean."

"Do you think you can do it?"

"Yes, Sir. I will not guarantee anything, but I think I may be able to do it."

So he led the way to the Elevator which we took to the 5th floor where the Advanced Optics Lab was located. As we left my Lab I picked up a straight pin from the desk near the door. In the Optics Lab Professor Trainer had left a Mercury lamp running and had a green filter in place to give me just green light from the 5462 Ångström line of the Mercury Spectrum. The light was focused properly on the interferometer.

Professor Trainer had made a good start, even if it had taken him the best part of four hours to do it! So I turned off the room lights, sat down in front of the interferometer, held the pin in the incoming beam of light, and saw three images of the pin, just as I expected. I found the correct adjusting screw by trial and error and moved it a tiny fraction of a turn until the three images were at the same height. This screw, with a pitch of about 30 threads/cm, rotated the interference plate around a horizontal axis.

Then I switched to the other adjusting screw which rotated the plate around a vertical axis and adjusted it until all three images of the pin coincided, and **BOOM,** there were all of the circular interference fringes! Professor Trainer saw me moving my head up and down, from side to side and along 45 degree diagonals and asked what I was doing.

"Just checking the ring system to be sure the plane of the second interferometer plate is oriented properly. There, that should do it; would you care to take a look Professor Trainer?"

I got out of the chair and he slipped in, took one look and exploded, "**GOOD GOD PHELPS, HOW IN KHOO**[73] **DID YOU DO THAT?**"

"Well, Professor Trainer, I ask that very same question about 20 times while you are working one Physics problem on the blackboard for us. I just had to adjust the interferometer plate so it was correctly oriented." He was shaking his head as I left the Lab and went back to my work in the basement.

Not long thereafter the Dean walked in and said, "Professor Trainer came to my office. What on earth did you do to him?"

"I just helped him align the Michelson Interferometer for his Optics Lab this afternoon. He couldn't find the fringes."

"Well that's two Theorists you have put to shame. Your answer to Professor Betts was a classic.[74] How are the spacers coming?"

"Pretty well, Sir. Nick did an incredible job on the invar spacers, and I have learned that if I use distilled water and cerium oxide under the low boss, 175 grit aluminum oxide under the high boss, and use the low boss as a pivot, I can rotate a spacer back and forth five times on each end and remove about 2500 Ångströms of invar from the high bosses. I finished the ½ cm spacer in about three days and the 1 cm spacers in less than a day. I think the 2.5, 5, 10, and 20 cm spacers will go quite quickly, probably an hour or two apiece. I do not think I will need pressure rods to do the final alignment with any spacer. Nick is machining the holders right now."

As Professor Newbound left the Lab he said, "I think I shall go have a little further talk with Professor Trainer."

It is always very satisfying to tweak a Theorist by doing something he cannot do! And I suspect the Dean was rather pleased to have a Full Professor deflated a little by **his** Graduate Student. No Graduate Student is supposed to be able to do that!!

---

[73] The key to decrypting **Bad Words** is explained in the footnote in the story "High School Chemistry."

[74] Betts – See the story "Candidacy Exam."

47. Endowed Scholarships

The University of Alberta has recognized that endowed scholarship funds are a great continuing need, and, as the cost of tuition, room and board and books continues to rise, many potential Students are simply priced out of the market for a University Degree and their talents and contributions to scholarship in their field of interest and to the Province of Alberta and the Dominion of Canada, and the rest of the world will be lost because they never had a chance to make them.

Therefore, the University has established the **Quae Cumquevera Society (What So Ever Things are True)** to recognize those individuals who do what they can for the University of Alberta, and leave a bequest in their estate plans. An Endowed Scholarship Fund will make a real difference to generations of Students. I hope that this book will inspire others to join the Society.

After Professor Newbound died, his four children established **"The Kenneth Bateman Newbound Memorial Physics Scholarship Endowment**," which I trust will assist many future Physics students to reach their goals.

Figure 1 (Above): Fritz and sister Margaret feeding ducks in Florida while they recovered from whooping cough.

Figure 3 (Above): "Let Fritz Do It" was one of his first entrepreneurial adventures.

Figure 2 (Above): Fritz wearing a cardboard box due to falling off the dock at Curtis, MI too often.

Figure 4 (Above): Fritz's senior year at Carleton College.

Figure 5 (Left): Fritz and Marion's wedding.

Figure 6 (Below): Fritz making bread with his son, Fred.

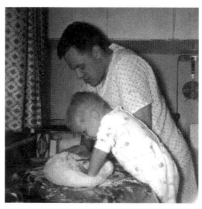

Figure 7 (Above): Cutting the cake at the wedding.

Figure 8 (Above): Fritz reading to Fred and Dorothy.

Figure 9 (Above): Fritz graduating from the University of Alberta with a Ph.D. in Physics.

Figure 10 (Above): Fritz, Marion, Fred and 6 week old Dorothy camping in Jaspan National Park.

Figure 11 (Above): Fritz mudding the ceiling in the house he built.

Figure 12 (Left): The (mostly) finished house that Fritz and Marion currently reside in.

Figure 13 (Right): Aerial shot of the Phelps Residence.

Figure 14 (Below): Fritz and his favorite blond, Ginger.

Figure 15 (Above): Scout Summer Camp Staff, Bear Lake (1978).

Figure 16 (Right): Fritz being awarded his Silver Beaver (1987).

Figure 17 (Below): Christmas with the family.

Figure 18 (Above): Family picture as a grandparent. Back row: Fred IV, Marion, Fritz, Rick. Front row: Li Li with Wu Hao, Mildred Riley (Marion's mother), and Dorothy.

Figure 19 (Above): The four Freds.

Figure 20 (Above): The lovebirds.

Figure 21 (Above): Commodore Fritz and the Old Sea Dog, Lacy, borrowed from Professor Scheide for VBS.

Figure 22 (Right): Fritz and his son, Rick, outside of Kalamazoo College.

Figure 23 (Left): Fritz sitting on a Lime (Stone) Pie in Three Rivers, Wisconsin on his way to 60th Carleton College Reunion.

Figure 24 (Right): Fritz and three of his senior year roommates at the Carleton 60th Reunion. L to R: Brace Anderson, Fritz, Obert Undem and Bob Patoff.

Part VIII. Family Stories (1960-Present)

48. Trains, Sugar Water, and Other Things

Fred was just nine months old when we left Detroit and drove to Edmonton, Alberta in Canada so that I could begin my Ph.D. Program at the University of Alberta. Someone had bought him a small Skaneateles wooden train which we set up on the living room floor of our apartment. He drove it around for hours on end. When Dorothy joined our family in July of 1962,[75] it was clear that Mφm needed a few minutes alone every week with Dorothy when she would not have her two boys underfoot.[76]

The solution was obvious. Freddy and I just got in the ***BIG GREEN CAR*** and drove to a railroad crossing close to where we lived. Then we parked by the crossing and waited for the Canadian National Transcontinental Passenger Train to drive by on its way to Vancouver, British Columbia. Every week we waved at the Train Engineer and all the passengers. After a couple weeks Freddy wanted to count the train cars, so we began.

Then I discovered that there was a huge train yard on the North Side of Edmonton, so we would drive out there and count the cars on the long freight trains that came from both East and West. The longest train we ever saw came from Vancouver, and I think it must have hauled wheat from the prairies to a bulk terminal on the coast because the side doors were open on each car. It started with three engines on the front, followed

---

[75] Fritz and Marion's second child and only Daughter, Dorothy, was actually born on June 17th. Her Mother confirms that she was only in the hospital for two days.
[76] Mφm's "two boys" were her Son and Husband. Rick, their second Son, came later.

by 150 empty box cars, then three more engines, another 150 empty cars and finally three pusher engines. So nine engines and 300 empty cars! It had to be a wheat train; what else could it be?

It was so exciting to count such a long train that we celebrated by stopping at an A & W Root Beer Drive-In and bought baby mugs of root beer that cost five cents each. Daddy was in trouble when we got home because Freddy did not want any lunch: He was full of sugar water. Mφm, who was later given the name of "Detective Mφm" by Dorothy, smelled a rat, and wanted to know what we had eaten?

"Just a five cent root beer at A & W."

I do not remember whether it was that night or later when we had green beans for supper, and Freddy did not want to eat his. So I lined them up on his plate and told him, "*do not eat the locomotive or any of the passenger cars.*" You never saw green beans disappear so fast; gobble, gobble, gobble they went down the hatch with a two-meter wide grin and both fists working as fast as was humanly possible. So Dad learned a good lesson on how to get a small boy to eat his peas or corn or anything else he did not really want. Just tell him to not eat it, and for sure, "*do not eat the train!*"

I am afraid all that counting and root beer gave Freddy **Permanent Head Damage,** or in the vernacular, a Ph.D. in Mathematics (or, to be a little more[77] exact, Mathematical Biology), under Professor Keener at the University of Utah, followed by a Post-Doc at Oxford at the Center of Mathematical Biology with Professor Murray. What is Mathematical Biology you ask? I will give you two examples from Fred's work.

---

[77] Technically this would be a little less exact because the Ph.D. was in "Applied Mathematics," although the applications in the thesis were biological.

49. Fred IV's Mathematical Biology — The Sex of Crocodilians[78]

Did you know that the sex of a Crocodile or an Alligator is determined by the temperature at which the eggs are incubated? The mother Croc or Alligator crawls up onto a levy, a strip of land with channels of water on each side. Mother Croc scoops out a shallow hole and lays several layers of eggs. The eggs in the bottom layer, which are in touch with the damp sand, hatch at about 30°C, and all are females. Higher levels, which incubate at about 32°C, hatch out to be males. Why? I don't have a clue, but there are about 10 females for each male Croc.[79]

50. Fred IV's Mathematical Biology — Visceral Leishmaniasis

There had been a serious outbreak of Leishmaniasis, a protozoan parasite of the Leishmania genus. This disease is the second-largest parasitic killer in the world, after malaria. Six Biologists from Princeton University went to Brazil to see what could be done to stop the epidemic, and all six of them caught the disease,[80] which is spread by the sand fly.

---

[78] The original document has the wonderful variant "Crockadilians."

[79] Phelps, F. *Optimal sex ratio as a function of egg incubation temperature in the crocodilians*. Bull. Math. Biol. 1992 Jan; 54(1):123-48. In Fred IV's paper, the assumptions were that, "male fitness depends more strongly on quality of incubation environment than female fitness, and that there is a strong correlation between a female's egg incubation temperature choice and the temperature at which she herself was incubated." Make an assumption that sex ratio as a function of incubation temperature is subject to evolutionary pressure and find what it evolves to.

The people who were catching the disease along the Amazon River were the **RICH INDIANS** who owned a dog and a few chickens. The natural host in the jungle is the fox. Domestic dogs are sufficiently genetically similar to foxes so that they can be the host. However, according to the Biologists, while chickens can supply blood to the flies, they are so genetically different that they cannot host the disease.

Let's think about how the disease progresses from one infected fly to a host and back to a new fly. Let's make the most simple-minded assumptions possible: that the flies are *equally ready* to bite any of the potential blood sources (excluding humans our purposes here), and that the *disease always* spreads between dogs and flies if either the dog or the fly is infected.

Suppose the Rich Man has one dog and nine chickens. 10% of the time an infected fly will bite the dog and spread the disease. But 90% of the time the fly bites a chicken and the disease does not spread.

Now assume the dog is infected. In order for the disease to spread back to a new fly, an uninfected fly must bite the infected dog. This happens 10% of the time – the other 90% of the time the fly bites chickens. Putting the two stages together, the cycle is completed $(10\%)^2$ or 1% of the time.

Now suppose the Rich Man has one dog and 99 chickens. Then the probability of completing the cycle becomes $1\%^2 = 0.01\%$. Therefore, one way to slow the disease is to have one dog and 99 chickens rather than one dog and nine chickens.

---

[80] This makes a good story, and Fritz insists that his son told him this. However, Fred IV has no recollection of reporting such an event and strongly doubts its authenticity. The rest of the presentation was also garbled, but has been thoroughly edited so that some truth does break through from time to time.

This was Fred's contribution: to realize that increasing the ***chicken to dog ratio*** may be one method of decreasing the incidence of disease. The Biologists were not impressed, citing the fact that more chickens meant more flies. The Math showed, however, that the presumed increase in the incidence of disease due to an increase of flies was overwhelmed (at least under the most simple-minded assumptions about fly behavior as described here) by the diluting effect of more bites going to the permanently disease-free chickens, because the diluting effect was "squared."

Unfortunately the Princeton[81] Biologists would not give Fred their primary data. If they had, he could have made much more progress, but of course you cannot give away your primary data because the person you give it to may publish an important result before you do. This is a clear case of a choice between, "give away your data and let the mathematicians publish while you perish" (because you lack one publication for promotion), or "ignore the Math, publish yourselves, and let the Indians perish."[82]

---

[81] I don't think any of the actual Biologists had any ties to Princeton and this was at Oxford. They certainly were not drawn from the almost certainly apocryphal **Group of Six** who had gotten the disease when they went to investigate.

[82] Truer version: Despite the rhetoric here, the project was collaborative. Fred asked for the data, and it took a long time to obtain, but he did eventually get enough of it to show that there was a **significant decrease in the disease rate** in villages as the chicken to dog ratio increased. The paper was never published. The closest thing to it is probably Courtenay O, Macdonald DW, Lainson R, Shaw JJ, Dye C. *Epidemiology of canine leishmaniasis: a comparative serological study of dogs and foxes in Amazon Brazil.* Parasitology. 1994 Sep; 109 (Pt 3):273-9.

51. Fred's Early Speech

A. North Saskatchewan River

Mφm left us for a few days while she was in the University of Alberta Hospital delivering Dorothy. We decided to have a picnic lunch in a park on the North side of the North Saskatchewan River. Fred (2.5 years old at the time), practiced saying the name of the River two or three times until he had it down perfectly.

Later we stopped by the Hospital to see Fred's new tiny little sister girl. Mφm asked Fred what we had been doing and he told her, "We had a picnic near Groat Road on the *North Side of the North Saskatchewan River.*" Such big words from such a small boy were wonderful to hear, and quite blew away the nurses!

B. New Pesser-Bound

One day, when Fred was about three years old, I decided to take him to the "Big Red Building" where Daddy worked. We visited the Spectroscopy Lab and looked at Daddy's wonderful toys and learned what some of them did.

We went to the Physics Department Shop and watched the Instrument Makers machining brass, invar and other metals. They were making equipment needed by the Graduate Students and the Professors who were doing Experimental Physics. A giant precision lathe was being used by Head Instrument Maker, Nick Riebeck, to make spacers for Daddy's interferometers.

Then we saw the Wood Shop where Daddy had made two little blue chairs 22 cm high, from scraps of plywood, and a little table 92 cm long by 59 cm wide, where Fred and Dorothy could sit facing each other while they drew pictures ad infinitum. I did not realize at the time that Fred was teaching Dorothy to lip read while they sat facing each other.

Then we took the big elevator to the 4th floor and walked to Professor Newbound's office so I could introduce Fred to him. I said, "Fred, say 'How do you do, Professor Newbound?'"

Fred put his hands on his hips and, with a big grin on his face, said, "How do you do, *New Pesser-Bound?*"

"Fred I think we need to practice that a little. Say, "Pro fess or" (pro fess or) "New" (new) "bound" (bound). Now let's put it all together. Say, "How do you do Professor Newbound."

And of course Fred said it perfectly, whereupon Professor Newbound's smile wrapped all the way around his head. Of course I had to say "Fred, that was perfect; you are such a good boy. Daddy is proud of you."

C. A VISIT TO WALLA WALLA

The second Christmas we were in Edmonton, we drove to Spokane. From there we made a trip to Walla Walla to see the Dean of Whitman College, who wanted me to leave Graduate School and teach Math and Physics for him. I declined.

In Walla Walla we stayed with my cousin Susie Taggart (Aunt Peg's daughter). At lunch one day, Fred took a banana from a bowl on the table, held it out and said, "Aunt Susie, please take the epidermis off this *Musa sapientum* for me." Her three kids had no idea what Fred had asked her to do and were looking rather stunned. Susie, who had an extensive scientific background, was doubled up at the sink, laughing. She explained that Fred had asked her to peal the banana but used the correct scientific names for both the skin and the banana. Not too shabby for a Two Year Old.

D. UNIVERSITY OF ALBERTA FOOTBALL

I have always enjoyed football games and found that, if we came at half time, Fred and I could watch the Golden Bears for free. So we attended numerous U. of A. football games together. I would take Fred's stroller. He had a nice view of the game and I would sit in the front row of seats.

There is a play called a "single" in Canadian Football in which a single point may be scored by kicking the ball over the back line of the end zone. After one such play Fred loudly asked, "Why are all those big men lying down on top of each other?" There were probably 150 spectators who heard him, including a faculty member or two from the Physics Department. They all stated laughing and watched Fred quite intently until the end of the game.

52. Stories of Dorothy

A. Favorite Bird

I thought the purpose of daughters was to give Daddy someone to tease, so when Dorothy asked over and over and over again, "Daddy, what is your favorite Bird," I always answered, "**BIG BIRD.**"

Her response was always the same: "Do you mean a California Condor"?

"No, I mean **Big Bird.**"

"Do you mean an Albatross?"

"No, I mean **Big Bird.**"

This continued for months, until eventually Rick had had enough and intervened, "Dorothy, do you remember Sesame Street and **BIG BIRD?**"

Her response was "Oh pfutt, you are the *Funniest Father* I ever had!!!"

B. Skinney Street

There is a street in Mount Pleasant with the name of South Kinney Street, but the street sign was missing a dot after the "S," and so it read S Kinney St., or obviously "SKinney Street." I kept telling Dorothy about "Skinny Street," but she never believed that there was such a thing. We went around and around about this for several months.

Then one day when we were traveling East on High Street, I told Dorothy to watch the street signs carefully. She finally saw, "Skinney Street." Her reaction was similar to when she finally understood who Big Bird was: "Oh, pfutt. Hahahahahahahaha," for several blocks.

C. YOU NEED MORE PRACTICE!

When Dorothy obtained her driver's license, I rode into town with her on High Street, and, on a yellow light, she turned left onto Main Street in front of an oncoming car. Fortunately, we were not T-boned, because the other driver was alert. Something about the way she was driving may have alerted him to the fact that something was not quite right.

She said, "**Oops**."

After I had zuxqj[83] out my underwear, I said, "You need more practice before you can drive." She recognized I was right and never complained until several months had passed when she asked, "How can I practice driving if I never get to drive?"

"I haven't been able to figure that one out either."

"Oh, pfutt."

But she was much more alert and careful after the delay. Mission accomplished.

---

[83] Fritz's Wife demanded that we take out this sentence, but we have chosen to encrypt a portion of it. Although reader discretion is advised, the key to decryption is explained in the footnote in the story "High School Chemistry." The original document used the charming variant "uxqj."

53. Richard

My second son, Rick, is five years younger than his brother Fred, and was always inspired to do everything his brother was doing. When Fred was old enough to join a Scout Troop, Rick was old enough to join a Cub Scout Pack. The first Scout Troop Fred joined was Troop 648, which met at Vowels Elementary School.

At first I made the assumption that the Troop was sponsored by the School PTA[84], but it was actually sponsored by The Church Of Jesus Christ of Latter Day Saints or "the Mormons." To stay involved, I joined the troop Committee and promptly was elected Committee Chairman, probably because I was the only adult to ask questions or offer ideas of things for the Troop to do.

Good Mormons have a supply of food at home that will last the family two full years. One commodity they emphasize is home storage wheat. When I found this out, I ordered 20 bags of Turkey Red Wheat (an excellent hard wheat) the next time they had a semi load from Idaho.

We had to drive to Midland to pick up our wheat, and I took Rick with me. On the way to Midland, we talked about the Upper Peninsula of Michigan, and Rick, who may have been five or six at the time, stuck his head out of the window and looked up, trying to see it! It was not there.

We have ground the wheat for many years, and have had wonderful whole wheat flower in bread and pancakes.

---

[84] Parent-Teacher Association

54. Scoutmaster of Troop 628

When we moved to Mount Pleasant, Fred was 10 years old, and had previously started in the Cub Scout Program while we lived in Rochester, New York, so it was natural to look for a Cub Pack he could join. We found one at his School. The advantage of this Pack was that he knew a few of the boys who were already in the Pack, especially his friend Greg Richardson.

As soon as Fred joined Greg's Den, an intense rivalry developed to see who could earn the most awards before the next monthly Pack meeting where awards were given in a sort of miniature Court of Honor. Greg was a little older and quickly earned his Arrow of Light, the highest award a Cub can earn, and left the Pack to join Troop 648. Fred immediately started to earn all 15 Webelos pins and his Arrow of Light. Webelos means, "We'll be loyal Scouts."

Fred turned 11 on the 7th of January 1971 and left the Cub Pack to join Troop 648 and Greg's Patrol. The boys had developed a competitive spirit in the Pack and it kicked into high gear in the Troop. A boy must complete about 20 projects to earn a Webelos pin or a merit badge. Fred and Greg often worked on merit badges together and they pushed each other to do better and better work at each step of the way.

Fritz was asked to become Pack Treasurer and quickly became Chairman of the Pack Committee, and then Chairman of the Troop Committee, probably because he was the only parent to ask questions at Committee meetings! And, he always had ideas of things for the boys to do. It was easy to have great ideas because he would just ask Fred and Greg what they would like to do. Then it was only a matter of figuring out how to implement the plan, allowing for the youngest Cubs to participate with the oldest boys and have fun doing it.

But that is easy too; you just ask the older boys how to include all the boys in the Troop. If they had a good idea you just said, "Wonderful idea; now do it." So the older boys have a stake in every project, and they do not want to lose face by failing, so they work very hard to gain the recognition and respect of the younger boys. The older boys are learning how to be Leaders and the younger Scouts now have Heroes to look up to, and they cannot let their older Scout friends down, so they work harder also.

Both boys advanced rapidly through the Scout ranks and eventually Fred became Senior Patrol Leader (SPL), which meant that it was up to him to be the Leader of the Patrol Leaders and plan all the details of each weekly meeting. Apparently the Scoutmaster and the Troop Committee members did not understand how to have a good Troop, and began to undercut the SPL. It therefore became necessary to start a new Scout Troop, Troop 200π, or, if you are not a Mathematician, Troop 628.

Fritz became Scoutmaster, a position he held for 34 years while 34 boys reached the Eagle Scout rank. Each Eagle was well and truly earned. Over those 34 years several boys abandoned the climb to Eagle because the Scoutmaster (SM) would not accept a merit badge that Mom had earned while she was trying to push her Son to the rank of Eagle.

I remember one Scout who showed up with penny, nickel, dime and quarter coin books to present for his Coin Collecting Merit Badge, but a couple questions showed that he really knew nothing about U.S. coins. I asked him where he got the coin books.

"My Mom went to the bank and came home with bags of coins and sat at the kitchen table all weekend looking through the bags for the coins needed to fill up the books."

"Well, how would you feel about me signing the Coin Collecting Merit Badge application, and at the Court of Honor we call your Mom up and give her the badge?"

"NO! My Mom would be so embarrassed she'd die!"

"So what do you want to do?"

"I think I'll go home and do the work myself."

A month or two later he knew more about coinage than I did! He knew about Greek coins, Roman Talents, Spanish Pieces of Eight, British coins and the Pound Sterling (actually a troy-pound of silver, which Sir Isaac Newton created while he was Master of the Mint). As far as I as was concerned, the most important thing was that the Scout had the satisfaction of knowing he had done the work himself.

55. A Very Smart Blond[85] Named Ginger

One of my Eagle Scouts came to my front door one day. When I answered the knocker, John said, "Dr. Phelps would you like a puppy?"

"Can I see them first?"

"No; they're not born yet."

My Wife said, "**OH! NO!** We're getting a dog; I hate dogs! I demand a family vote!"

The vote was 4 votes against and 1 vote in favor, so we got the dog[86] and Mφm named her Ginger. After considerable mumbling and protests I said to my children, "If you don't like my dog, you don't have to stay here. Feel free to move out; there are sleeping bags and tents in the

---

[85] With the encouragement of Fritz's Grandson, the editor has chosen to retain the author's charming spelling here and everywhere.

[86] Recently someone discovered an authentic list of pros and cons about getting the dog, written in Dorothy's handwriting. The pros: "barkless, friendly, cute, walks – good exercise for YOU!" The cons: "expensive, shots, license, spay, cat intolerance, bathroom all over the lawn, walks – tracks in lots of mud – big feet, food, smell, baths, may get old, can't travel, Mφm doesn't want to take care of it, WE don't want it!"

Attic and Coleman stoves in the Garage, but if you move out, don't expect me to pay for College." It is remarkable how quickly people can change their minds when the facts of a situation are explained in **Simple Declarative Sentences**.

I think Dorothy summed it up best, "I, I, I think I like dogs." Then that brat girl stole my puppy by putting a chair beside her bed so Ginger could jump up onto the bed and sleep with her. I was mad: Ginger was warm and soft and I wanted to sleep with her! I did for about a week, and then my Wife said, "What are these red spots on my legs that itch like crazy?"

"Oh, you mean like the red spots on my legs?"

"Yes."

"I think they are flea bites."

"Get that gdpq[87] dog out of my bed, **NOW!!**"

Ginger was 3/4 Cocker Spaniel and ¼ Dachshund, but she looked like a Cocker that was 4 cm closer to the road and 10 cm longer from the tip of her wet nose to the tip of her tail than her Mother, "Peaches." Because she was a BLOND, Dr. Phelps knew she would be exceptionally **SMART**, and started to teach her Physics from the age of seven weeks.

For Ginger's first Christmas, Dorothy had given me a bath towel with Paw Prints and the name **GINGER** embroidered on it, and a Paw Print rubber stamp. Keep reading to see why this was so important.

---

[87] The key to decrypting **Bad Words** is explained in the footnote in the story "High School Chemistry."

56. THE AMANA COLONIES, IOWA

Mφm and I had driven to California one summer to see Dorothy and Andy.[88] On the way home we stopped at the Amana Colonies in Iowa to buy Gasoline. Because they did not have pay-at-the-pump I had to go into the little shop, and when I entered, I was confronted with hundreds of meters of 7 cm deep shelving, holding thousands of coffee mugs on them. Each mug had a picture of a dog. **WOW**, how neat is that?

I had looked at perhaps 50 mugs when the girl that ran the shop came to see what I was doing.

"What kind of a dog are you looking for?"

"A dog that is 3/4^{ths} Cocker Spaniel and 1/4th Dachshund."

She put her hands on her hips and asked, "What on earth would you call a mutt like that?

"I call her Ginger."

"**Oh, no**! Now I'm in trouble," and she started to walk away.

She was probably in her late 30's and a fairly decent looking blond. So I had to say, "Do you know another name for a smart blond?"

She whipped around and said, "O.K., let me have it!"

"Ginger."

"**Oh no**, now I am in really deep trouble. I don't suppose I make a sale today?"

"Probably not, but if you would like to meet Ginger I will go to the car and get her for you."

"No, its O.K." Then she asked, "Are there any others?"

"Sure there are lots of smart blonds in the world."

"There are? Who are they?"

"You have hundreds right here in your shop!"

---

[88] Dor's Husband, whom she met at the age of three, at Rackham School for the Deaf.

"I do?"

"Sure, Yellow Labs, Golden Retrievers and Blond Cocker Spaniels."

"Oooooh, I've never been in such deep trouble before!" she exclaimed as she put her head on the counter.

We dove on towards Mount Metropolis.[89]

57. THE BAT

Our house in Mount Pleasant is one I built mostly by myself, starting in the summer of 1971, with help from three of my Students each of whom had some building experience. We managed to get the first story up and the second story, which is a huge Attic. We finished the roof sheathing, added tar paper and some of the shingles, until an Ice Storm on Thanksgiving drove me off the roof until the next spring. But there was plenty of work (plumbing and wiring) to do inside during the winter.

Many bats live in our vicinity, and only need a hole the size of a pencil to gain entrance. One evening a bat began flying through the kitchen. Fortunately, the kitchen sink with garbage disposer was installed and working. Several loud screams brought me running, and I continued into the Garage to grab a badminton racket.

After several attempts, the bat sustained a mighty wallop, and landed in the sink. The entrance to the garbage disposer was open, so when I used my fearsome badminton racket to push him to the edge of the precipice, the bat continued his journey to the happy hunting ground. He tumbled neatly into the disposer. One second later the plug was in

---

[89] This is Dr. Phelps' moniker for Mount Pleasant, Michigan.

place, the cold water was running full force, and a flick of the motor switch started his demise.

How could I be so cruel? Well bats sometimes are carriers of rabies, and while I did not know about this one, "safe" is much better than "sorry."

We have a new bat visitor every few years. I made a huge butterfly net to catch them. Swinging the net always alerts their acoustical radar set when they fly by, so I just hold the net steady and wait for the bat to hit the bottom of the net which I then roll over a couple times, trapping him inside. Then it is only necessary to run outside, unwind the butterfly net, dumping the bat on the ground. He can stay there until he is able to fly, and I am safely inside, sitting in a chair or lying on the davenport, while my heartbeat slows to normal.

58. Tahquamenon Falls and the Great Lakes Shipwreck Museum

One year when Fred and family were in town, Fred wanted to go to the Upper Peninsula to see a couple lighthouses and Tahquamenon Falls. We loaded our minivan and headed North.

There are actually two sets of falls on the Tahquamenon river and there is a wooden walkway between them which is about 1.6 km long paved with 2x4's. We had all walked to the upper falls, including Ginger. The views were spectacular, and it is easy to see why many tourists call the upper falls the "Tea Falls," because all the tannin in the water makes the river look like freshly brewed tea.

On the way back to the parking lot I saw a young girl coming towards us and looking bug-eyed at Ginger. She stopped, pointed towards my puppy and inquired in a very loud voice, "What is **That Thing**?"

Her question took me by surprise and I replied, "I think she is a dog."

The girl started to laugh and, still pointing at Ginger, said, **"Look Mommy, that thing is a DOG!"** Out of the mouths of babes.... I still laugh every time I think of her and wonder what her name was and what did she think I had on my leash, a stupid CAT?

Oh yes, the Great Lakes Shipwreck Museum has a large Second Order Fresnel Lens from the Whitefish Point Light Station. I had heard about them years ago and include a brief discussion of their optical properties in my class whenever I teach Optics, but I had never seen one. Do not pronounce the "s" in Fresnel: It is French and sounds like "frenel." So the tour was an educational experience for me!!!

After leaving Whitefish Point we travelled West on a dirt road (starting on MI-412) towards Grand Marais and eventually reached Muskellunge State Park where there was a nice beach and a clean, unused campground.[90] Lake Superior was exceptionally warm, out to at least 100 meters from shore, and Fred took his three children swimming in the big waves while I rolled Ginger on her back on a picnic table and used my Swiss Army Knife scissors to cut knots of hair from between the pads on her feet. She had been limping and I did not like it. I had to be very careful not to pull the hairs. It took about ½ hour for each Paw, but she never whimpered and was a happy puppy when I let her down to run a bit on the beach.

---

[90] Editor: I don't think the locations are accurate. I believe the swimming was near Twelve Mile Beach Campground, to the West of Grand Marais and the campsite was also elsewhere.

59. Dorothy Meets Her Husband

Dorothy, just remember God can make something **GOOD** out of something that initially appears bad. After I finished my thesis exam, I went on a long trip and visited two colleges in California, the Colorado School of Mines and the U. of Michigan. Naturally I checked out the programs for deaf children at each stop.

I DID NOT LIKE what I found in California. I thought the programs for the deaf were terrible, and the people running them completely incompetent. The school for the deaf in Denver was better, but there was just a feeling that it was not right. I turned down what seemed to be a nice offer from the School of Mines because each Physics faculty member seemed to be at odds with every other Professor in the Department and because of the School for the Deaf.

While I was gone, Mφm packed up you and Fred and headed to Detroit on the Canadian Pacific Train and I took a red-eye flight from Denver to Metro. We were there for Christmas. Grandpa loaned me a car and I drove out to Ypsilanti to the Rackham School for the Deaf and then to the U. of M. for an interview with the Institute of Science and Technology (IST). I decided Miss Murrow at the School for the Deaf was *wonderful* and had an *excellent program*. Next IST offered me a research job at 11K/annum. So I told the Rackham School we would be there in the fall, and accepted the job at the U. of M.

I think it was a year later when I went with Mφm to the George School for some program and there was some *evil little boy* sitting **NEXT TO MY DAUGHTER AND HOLDING HER HAND**. Hum, this could prove to be serious. That was part of the reason I wanted to throw up my hands and shout **HALLELUJAH** as you and that *evil boy* walked down the aisle after your wedding! Thanks Andy for taking her off of my hands. She is tolerable for a week or two but a whole lifetime??? Andy, you must be as tough as **ATLAS**, or at least have the heart of **a SAINT!**

I really wanted a teaching job and eventually got one at the Detroit Institute of Technology, but it was only 2/3^{rds} time and I really needed a larger income. I was offered a job as Head of Diffraction Grating Research at Bausch & Lomb and we moved to Rochester, N.Y. where they seemed to have an outstanding School for the Deaf.

But I still wanted a teaching job. Dr. McDermott made annual offers to me from CMU and while I thought the program for Deaf Children was inadequate, God made it quite clear that that was where He wanted me because every other possible door slammed shut. I was promised a Lab and startup funds but never had either and so a series of Deans and Provosts decided I was worthless because I refused to publish nonsense in *The Journal of Irreproducible Results*. Year after year promotion to Professor was denied on some trumped-up nonsense, and eventually I decided that I would concentrate on helping my Pre-Med Students prepare for their M-CAT exams, and that has been most satisfying. Every day I still wish I were teaching, but I am sure that is part of God's Plan too...

To quote Great Uncle John: "Oh, Woe is me!" My blond died of Old Age and someone[91] acts like the fifth of Snow White's seven friends,[92] but she did confess that she is afraid she would trip over a new puppy, fall on her and kill her with the impact and that would break my heart. If that happened, I think I could quit crying within a month or two, but it is best to NOT HAVE TO FIND OUT BY EXPERIMENT.

---

[91] i.e., Marion.
[92] i.e., Happy.

Part IX. Professor at Central Michigan University (1970-2012)

60. The True/False Exam

I was teaching physics at the Detroit Institute of Technology[93] and was scheduled to give a paper at the meeting of the American Astronomical Society (AAS) at the University of Victoria in British Columbia. The only trouble was that I had to give a final exam, grade it and submit final grades, and I had only two hours after the end of the exam to get to the airport to catch my plane to British Columbia.

I told the class about the time crunch, and had decided the only hope was to give them a True/False exam of 150 questions. I had to think up a way to speed up the grading, and hit upon the idea of making *all 150 answers True*. That way, in order to quickly grade the exams, I would have to only count up the False answers.

Several Really Good Students could not believe that every answer was *True*, and they hunted for a few False ones. When I returned to Detroit, a student named W. E. Capers said, "I really hunted for a False answer."

I reminded him that I had just two hours to grade the exams, calculate final grades, post them and get to Metro for my flight to British Columbia. I just counted the number of times each Student answered "False" ~~and subtracted from 150 to~~ calculate his final grade. The rest of

---

[93] Strictly speaking this story took place about 1968, before Fritz became a Professor at CMU. In 1964 the family moved to Ann Arbor, Michigan for five years where he had a variety of jobs, followed by a year in Pittsford, New York, where he worked at Bausch & Lomb in Rochester, New York. This is the only story from this period.

the work was already done and I only had to add a final grade to one number to get the semester total. It was hectic, but it worked! And I DID MAKE IT TO THE AAS MEETING on time.

61. MY ANTI-RHODES SCHOLAR

One year when I was teaching Physics at CMU, I had about the ***dumbest dodo*** in my Pre-Med class that I have ever encountered. He did not know right from wrong and thought the faculty should always give him high grades, just because he came to class. I had given an hour exam, and after I returned it, he came to my office to complain about his grade, which was 15%. Looking back, I cannot see what he had done to earn such a high grade.

He said, "Why did I get 15%; my girlfriend got 85%. I should get 85% too!"

"Why is that?"

"Because I copied her exam."

"Do you think it is smart to tell your Professor that you cheated on the exam?"

No answer, just a glare. So I continued, "I suppose that you did not notice that you had a different exam than your girlfriend?"

This time the response was instantaneous. A rather bitter, "Oh, you Vrq ri d Elwfk!!![94]"

My response was, "Do you really think it is smart to suggest that your Professors' Mother barked when he was born?"

---

[94] The key to decrypting **Bad Words** is explained in the footnote in the story "High School Chemistry."

Another glare. "If you wish to discuss this further, make an appointment with the Dean or the office of Student Life, and I shall prepare a letter asking him to expel you from CMU for plagiarism. I think you have the grade you earned."

He stomped out of my office quite angry.

62. Mr. Gormley

Jim Gormley was a superb High School Physics Teacher in Mount Pleasant, Michigan. I first met him in 1970, my first semester on the faculty of Central Michigan University. After I had used Serway and Faughn[95] for many years and through seven editions, Dr. Vuille became the lead author. I had written him a letter with a few suggestions of things I would like to see changed in the next edition. My letter vanished in the pile on his desk and came to light three years later. As you might expect he wrote and apologized for the delay in answering. This is my response:

Dr. Vuille,

Thanks for your letter. Most unfortunately I retired on August 15th, 50 years after I received my Ph.D. from the University of Alberta. It is awful to have no Pre-Med Students to prepare for their M-CAT exams. I am pleased that you found the letter from me, even if it was buried for three years. But I can top your story.

When I came to CMU in 1970 I was assigned to teach a graduate course in Theoretical Physics, even though I am an Experimentalist. There were seven MS Students in the class including Jim Gormley, our Mount Pleasant High School Physics Teacher.

---

[95] A College Physics textbook.

In 1980 some wag[96] said to me, "Dr. Phelps, what is the color of the top of your desk?"

"I don't know; I shall determine the answer by experiment."

So I started in and had thrown away four or five huge wastebaskets of papers, and had just discovered that my desk was green, when I heard Jim's voice in the hall. We had hired him to teach a Lab section for us. Shortly thereafter I found a set of his homework in my mess.

I thought, "This is too good an opportunity to pass up," and went down the hall to Jim's classroom. He was just starting to explain that week's experiment and demonstrating how to do it. When he looked up I handed him his paper and said, as gruffly as I could manage, "Mr. Gormley, if you want credit for your problems, you must submit them more promptly!" and I ran for the door.

*A voiced behind me bellowed, "**Good GOD**, I handed in these problems ten years ago and he still hasn't graded them!!!"*

After class Jim came to my office and said, "Can you still do them?"

"I don't know Jim, they are awful hard problems."

"You're telling me? I know; I struggled with them for days."

To this day, whenever I see Jim, the first thing he asks is, "Have you finished grading my problems?"

*"**NO**, Jim, they are way too hard for my atrophied brain."*

63. THE EMINENT INDIVIDUAL

The ballast resister in Fritz's Chrysler died in Edina, Minnesota as he and his Wife were about to cross into Canada on the way to his 1983 Sabbatical at the Dominion Astrophysical Observatory. Several letters had been exchanged between the Director of the Observatory and CMU and

---

[96] Wag: smart aleck.

Fritz thought all of the details were in place and properly noted for the benefit of the Canadian Emigration Authorities.

After the car was repaired, Fritz and Marion left Edina and headed for the border crossing between Portal, North Dakota and North Portal, Saskatchewan. The Canadian border agent asked where we were going and how long we would be in Canada. He seemed to be completely out of his league when Fritz told him, "the Dominion Astrophysical Observatory, near Victoria, British Columbia," and that they would be there for four months. He read all the papers offered and asked if Fritz would be paid for his work by the Observatory.

"No, Sir."

It was spelled out very explicitly that the work would not be compensated in any way with Canadian Dollars. So the poor guy started to paw through several books which detailed many different classifications under which people could be admitted to the Dominion of Canada, but none of them seemed to fit. Suddenly he had an **IDEA**.

"I could admit you as an **EMINENT INDIVIDUAL**; you are an **Eminent Individual**, aren't you?"

Fritz's answer was, "I think my Mother would agree with you that I am an **Eminent Individual,** but probably she is the only person on earth who would do so."

"Well, if your Mother, agrees with me, then that is the category I will use, and so I will admit you to the Dominion of Canada as an **Eminent Individual**. I have never met an **Eminent Individual** before; let me shake your hand and wish you a very pleasant stay in Canada.

After an hour or so at the border crossing, we were on our way to Les Roches Provincial Park where we planned to camp for the night. The next day we would drive to Regina and on to Edmonton for a short visit with Professor Newbound before we crossed the Rocky Mountains to Vancouver, and a ferry ride from Tsawwassen to Nanaimo, British

Columbia, and our new home for the next four months on Vancouver Island.

If the ballast resistor had died at Les Roches Provincial Park, how could we have gotten help? There were no cell phones in those days and it was past the camping season. I would not have known what to do, or how to fix the problem without a Mechanic telling me step by step do this, then do that. My Grandmother used to tell me, "God watches out for fools and old people, and I am not very old."

64. MUDDY PAW PRINTS IN PRE-MED PHYSICS

My Pre-Med Physics class is a tough, demanding, problem-solving course and most Pre-Med Students are not too happy about having to take it; however, a good grade is required for admission to all sorts of Medical programs, like MD (which I think means "Mule Doctor"), DO,[97] DVM,[98] Sports Medicine, Athletic Trainer, Dental School, Physical Therapy, and on and on it goes. The goal of this class is to help the Students learn enough Physics to pass their Medical College Admission Test (M-CAT), or the equivalent for their field of study, because if they do not pass their particular M-CAT, their career ends before it begins. Furthermore, high grades on the Physics questions of the M-CAT indicate to the Dean of Admission of any Medical School that this is a **Very Bright Student Indeed** and he should be admitted to the program.

Therefore, each week I assigned eight problems in all Pre-Med classes. With sections as large as 120, I would need to grade as many as 960 problems per week. At 2.5 minutes per problem it would take a paper

---

[97] Doctor of Osteopathic Medicine.
[98] Doctor of Veterinary Medicine.

grader working 40 hours per week to grade all of them, obviously an impossible situation. The solution chosen was to hire one or two paper graders.

The graders would grade only five problems for each Student each week. But solutions to all eight problems had to be submitted because we do not choose which problems to grade until we sit down to actually do the grading. If a Student earned 25/25 on the graded problems, I thought the Student should be rewarded somehow, so I began to write **Good Boy** or **Good Girl** on their papers.

After I had been writing **Good Boy** or **Good Girl** for several years, Jessica Morgan enrolled in my class. One day she came to my office and asked, "Dr. Phelps, why do you write **Good Boy** or **Good Girl** on our problem sets?"

"Well Jessica, when I take Ginger out in the morning and she does what I want her to do, I pet her a little bit and tell her she is a **Good Girl**, so I thought if you do what I want you to do and get a perfect grade of 25/25 on your problem set, I should also tell you **Good Boy** or **Good Girl**. It is sort of like a gold star for a kindergartener."

But Dr. Phelps, "Why did you write **Good Boy** on my paper?"

"Um, err, ah, ah, ah, well Jessica, Biology was never my favorite subject!"

"Oh, O.K."

As she left my office I sat there and thought, "I cannot use **Good Boy** or **Good Girl** if I cannot tell the **Boys** from the **Girls**! I must find something that is "gender neutral."[99] Then I saw the rubber Paw Print on my desk that Dorothy had given me. "**THAT'S IT! THAT'S WHAT I WILL USE!**"

---

[99] Finally, a useful purpose for this politically correct phrase.

So the next day I told the class Jessica had come to my office and asked me why I wrote **Good Boy** or **Good Girl** on their papers? The whole class laughed uproariously when I explained that I had written **Good Boy** on Jessica's paper and I would no longer write those phrases because I seemed unable to tell **Boys** from **Girls**. Why? "Because I do not understand Biology. There are way too many variables in Biology, and besides Biology was not my favorite subject and Ginger has come up with much better plan."

She said, "Daddy, I could put a muddy Paw Print on the papers of those Students that do the best work if that would help." So if you see a muddy Paw Print on your paper, you will know that you got 25/25 on a problem set or 10/10 on a quiz or 100% on an hour exam.

The Paw Prints were a tremendous hit and many Students almost cried when they did not receive a Paw Print on a returned assignment. Several Students asked if they were really Ginger's Paw Prints, and they seemed so sad when I told them it was actually a rubber stamp Dorothy had given me for Ginger's first Christmas, but I was so impressed with the result that I asked Jessica what the big deal was.

She said, "We know it only takes you a couple seconds to put a Paw Print on our papers, but it tells us you care, and that makes all the difference in the world to us."

I never thought of that possibility, probably because I am not a shrink!!! Every Monday I would tell the class what percentage had Paw Prints on the Thursday quiz and how excited Ginger was if she could put muddy Paw Prints on 85% of their papers or how sad she looked if she had to limit herself to stomping on less than 50% of the papers.

65. Professor Bromley and the Christian Faculty Lunch

Starting in the mid-1990s Professor Bromley formed the Christian Faculty Lunch which met weekly, every Wednesday, until about 2012. Sometimes we would just talk, sometimes just pray, or watch part of a DVD. One of the latter was "Molder of Dreams," by Guy Dowd. He taught English at Brainerd High School in Minnesota. Guy was **NATIONAL TEACHER OF THE YEAR** and was at the White House to receive his award from President Reagan the day the shuttle blew up. Guy was always sensitive to people's feelings. He closed his story by telling us that every Student comes to class with a mask on; all were hurting inside, but could not admit it to anyone.

"Couldn't we just acknowledge they exist? Couldn't we just give them a Birthday Card? As I walked back to class I thought about his closing remarks and what a **Great Idea** it was, but I am not going to spend $3.95 on a Hallmark card for each of my 200 Students. I would go bankrupt!

When Ginger was about eight or nine weeks old, Dorothy had taken a picture of her lying in my port[100] arm. The expression on Ginger's face said to me, "I think I've got it made here folks: All I have to do is let him pet my soft tummy with his starboard[101] hand."

One of the Graduate Students figured out how to scan the photograph and turn it upside down, so that when a short message was printed, the paper could be folded up correctly into a Happy Birthday Card. Ginger's message was, "**Daddy says he is busy grading papers,**

---

[100] Left?
[101] Right?

so I licked him on the chin to tell him I would send you a Happy Birthday Card. Love, Ginger." She signed it with a Paw Print.

Hummm. Let's try an experiment, we will print a few cards and see what happens.

I gave unused IBM Cards[102] to all of the Students in each of my classes and told them that on the back of the card they were to write the class designator, year and term, and on the next line, their name and birthdate, and then hand them in.

"Why Dr. Phelps?"

"Ginger is working on a new idea which I think you may like."

"Oh, O.K."

The first class to receive cards was a Lab section and the first recipient was a football lineman with shoulders at least one meter wide. So I attached a Birthday Card to his Lab report before I returned it. He stayed after class and was nearly in tears as he came to my desk. I said, "I hope I did not insult you with this card."

He said, "You will never know how much this means to me. This is the first Birthday Card I have ever gotten in my whole life; I am going to keep it forever."

The next week his two Lab Partners, both girls, had Birthdays and I attached Cards to their Lab reports. They both stayed after class to talk to me. Gulp, I wonder if I am in trouble with the Dean! I said again, "I hope I did not insult you with the cards; should Ginger change the sentiment?"

"Oh NO! Don't ever change a thing!!! The cards are perfect the way they are!"

---

[102] Cards whose purposes are explained in the section "Learning to Write Computer Programs." Dr. Phelps currently possesses thousands upon thousands of unused IBM cards leftover from his days in Edmonton; their primary function is for grocery lists.

66. Sarah

Sarah enrolled in my Pre-Med Physics class in about 1998. She came to class every day with her Black Lab, Mimi, and sat in the front row. She would sit very quietly and stare at the blackboard as though she was following everything I wrote there. Unfortunately she never mentioned to me that she had problems with her vision and I thought she could see a little bit because of how she looked at the blackboard, but she was not doing very well. Her quiz grades were a disaster and her problem sets had many mistakes.

I began asking her more and more questions and was stunned to learn during the 10th week of class that she did not even have a copy of the textbook in Braille,[103] so I went to the Handicapped Student office. They had one flown in, but the Publisher sent the wrong half of the book! Then Sarah told me she had tunnel vision in one eye but it was still hard to see the blackboard.

I tried to find a Tutor among the Physics Graduate Students with no luck. I could not find an Undergrad in Physics, Math or Computer Science who would take her on, even though the Physics Department would pay them for the tutoring. (I think potential Tutors thought if she failed it would be a reflection on them and they did not want to take a chance of damaging their own reputations.)

Finally, I told her I would have to tutor her myself. We met as often as we could for four weeks, but did not get too far. Some days we would do one homework problem and some days two or three. I learned that Sarah had had normal vision as a child, but the Doctors think one day a virus went up her spinal column and down her optic nerve and

---

[103] The original had "brail," which seems to be a sailing term.

destroyed her vision. She was O.K. when she went to bed that night, but in the morning it was like looking through waxed paper.

At the end of the semester I told Sarah I could not give her a passing grade because she did not know the material. Would she accept an incomplete grade and work with me in the fall to complete the course?

"YES!"

Then I said, "But this will violate University Policy on incomplete grades and I cannot do it unless the Department Chairman and Dean give me permission."

So I went to the Chairman and told him the story. When I mentioned that this would be a clear violation of University Policy, he said, "**DO IT ANYWAY.**" Then I made a trip to see the Dean and after hearing the same story he said, "**DO IT ANYWAY.**"

We worked every day. Sarah had some time that fall and by the middle of November she had solved all of the 125 problems I had assigned for the semester. With her tunnel vision, I could tell her to draw a Cartesian coordinate system with her **MARKS-A-LOT** and she would. Then I would have her put a spot on the paper. "Now stick your finger on the spot." Then I would take her finger and tell her that spot has a mass of 11.6 kg (Ginger of course), and she is running this way (and I would push her finger along the paper) with a velocity of 6.28 m/s at this angle θ relative to the X axis, and I would push her finger in an arc. "Now calculate Ginger's Momentum."

Her calculator would talk to her and tell her what she had entered and what the final answer was. Then I would tell her to calculate the X and Y components of Ginger's Momentum and she would say, "Oh, yes. I need the cosine of the angle for the X component," and she would calculate it, and so on. It was slow and painful work, but she learned that I would just sit there and say nothing unless she gave me the proper units and direction if the quantity was a vector.

With just four weeks left in the fall semester she finished all of the homework and all the quizzes and hour exams. Sarah said, "You told me if I finished all the problems and quizzes and tests I would have a B. ***But I have never worked so hard in my life and I want an A. What do I have to do for an A?***"

"Well you had only 15 points or so, on the final the first time; you will have to take it over again and do better."

"Will you help me?"

"Sure. I will read the problems to you." I do not remember having to push her finger around much on the paper for the final but I may have. The result was that Sarah got 300/250 on the final because I added a 50 point Extra Credit Problem.

"NOW DO I GET MY A?"

"SARAH, I THINK YOU HAVE EARNED IT."

"I KNOW I HAVE EARNED IT."

That girl continuously reminded me of my deaf Daughter Dorothy. Like Dor, she absolutely would not quit until everything was mastered. Her attitude was, **"So I can't see. That does not mean I cannot learn it. It just takes me longer to learn it, that's all."**

About two years later I saw Sarah and Mimi waiting for a bus. She had a big ring on her finger so I asked, "Sarah is that an engagement ring?"

"No, I got married and my Husband is in the Marines and he is in Afghanistan."

She had been admitted to the CMU Doctor of Physical Therapy program and the Dean had given her six years to finish a three year program. She is now a licensed Physical Therapist with an office in a small Michigan town and she has two Sons. Sarah is someone every CMU Student, Faculty Member and Administrator can be proud to number among our graduates.

67. Tensors and Ellen

Why do so many Students dread taking Physics, and why do they all think it is such a hard subject? After struggling to find the answer for many years, it hit me one day: The Mathematics we use in so many Physics problems is not the Mathematics the Students learn about in Grade School. The textbooks never tell them, and no Professor I ever had even mentioned the subject.

There are different classes of mathematical entities which go by the names of Tensors of Rank Zero, Tensors of Rank One, Tensors of Rank Two, and, as far as I know Tensors of Rank Three, Four, and higher.

Tensors of Rank Zero (also called scalars) are defined by a magnitude and a unit. The magnitude tells how many or how much and the unit tells you what you are talking about. And I would start a list on the board of several examples:

Examples of Tensors of Rank Zero (or Scalars)
- Mass: 3.14 kg
- Time: 15 sec
- Temperature: 9.36 °C
- Speed: 85.32 km/hr
- Kinetic Energy: 17.0 joules

These tensors can be written several different ways, all of which are equivalent. One year can be written as 12 months or 52 weeks, or 365.2242 days. Or 3.15×10^7 seconds. If we change the units then we must also change the magnitude.

As another example, 3.24 kg could be written 3240 gm or 0.00324 metric tonnes. The choice of units is up to you, but sometimes it is not a good idea to use certain units: Unless you want to get blipped on the head with a frying pan, I don't think you should state the mass of your Wife in tonnes. It would be much more diplomatic to use kilograms. However, in solving Physics problems in which you have to calculate some results, mass must always be measured in kilograms and time must be measured in seconds or the answer you get will not have the correct units.

Tensors of Rank One (Vectors) are defined by a magnitude, a unit, and a direction. The direction is just as important as the magnitude or the units and must always be stated in the answer if you want full credit. But the tendency is to forget to state the direction. You already know that some quantities must have a direction specified but probably no one has ever told you so.

Consider a car stuck in a snow bank. In one class I drew a snowbank on the blackboard and stuck a car, front first, in the snow. To get the car unstuck so I could continue driving to Central Magnificent University[104] for my 8 a.m. Physics class, I got behind the car and pushed on it with a force shown by an arrow pointing *INTO* the snowbank.

One of the Students, whose name was Ellen, shouted, "Dr. Phelps, **THAT'S STOOOOPID!**" Ellen seemed a little embarrassed by her out-burst so I said, "Ellen, you are absolutely right. It is very **STOOOOPID**. Are you trying to tell me the direction of the push is important?"

After some thought she replied, "Yes, that is exactly what I am trying to say."

"Well Ellen, you are absolutely right about that also. I knew that you already know these things, but I bet no one ever talked to you about them before." So we started a list of Tensors of Rank One.

Examples of Tensors of Rank One (or Vectors)
- Displacement
- Velocity

---

[104] Author's moniker for Central Michigan University.

- Acceleration
- Force
- Momentum
- Angular Momentum

The Students had to be aware of what type of tensor they were using and quickly realized why the direction must be specified where needed.

68. A Word on Diplomacy

As mentioned in the previous story, it is probably not a good idea to measure your Wife's mass in metric tonnes. But that reminded me of a talk given to the Student body of Carleton College in a College-wide convocation by President Lawrence McKinley Gould. He pointed out that you can say exactly the same thing in several ways and illustrated this with the following example: suppose you see the ugliest girl in the world. You could blurt out, **"You have a face that would stop a clock!!"** Or you could say exactly the same thing a little more diplomatically with, **"My dear, when I look at you time stands still."** This bit of advice from President Gould has stopped me on several occasions from saying something that I knew I would later regret. Thanks President Gould, for some really good advice.

69. Tiffany and Brother Stoneking

I shifted my 4th and 5th lumbar vertebrae while I was on the bayonet course in the Army and had back pains and cramps in my thighs and tingling legs for 13 years. Eventually I recovered, but I knew I had to be very careful, and not lift too much weight, or I would again squash the disc[105] that was displaced in my back.

Then in 1996, Mφm told me to pull the vines out of the shrubs at the front of the house, and, like a moron, I tried to do it. The pain was severe, just like the pain I had had forty years before when I ruined my back for the first time. It took me 40 minutes to walk up one flight of stairs to my office after my first class in the fall.

I rolled around Dow Hall in a wheelchair borrowed from Mount Pleasant Community Church. I could stand just long enough to write one line of an equation on the board. Then I had to sit again, because while I was standing, the pain just increased exponentially.

Some years before all of this, a student named Tiffany had enrolled in my Pre-Med Physics. While she was enrolled in the course, she frequently came to my office and told me little bits about herself. When she found I would listen and not pass judgement, she began to open up, and told me her Husband wanted a Party Girl who would get drunk every night and use drugs with him. She did not want that kind of life, but wanted someone to help take care of her three children. When she eventually found God and started preaching to her Husband, he divorced her.

She told me about an Itinerant Evangelist, Brother Stoneking, who came to the Pentecostal Temple in Midland each April. When Tiffany invited me to attend Brother Stoneking's "Up Lift" Conference that spring, I convinced Mφm to go with me. I was impressed with his stories, but Mφm did not like it at all, and would never go back to hear him preach. So, for several years, I went alone to hear Brother Stoneking when he was holding his annual "UP LIFT" Conference.

---

[105] The original spelling was, of course, disk.

After she graduated she would drop by once in a while to say hello. In 1996, after re-hurting my back, I rolled up to my office door in my wheelchair, and found that Tiffany had left a note for me, saying that Brother Stoneking would be in Midland that weekend. When I told Mφm I was going to miss our own Church's Care Group to hear Brother Stoneking, she did not raise her usual objections.

After two hours of Brother Stoneking's peaching, pandemonium often sets in, as people speak in tongues, run in circles, lie on the floor, or in general act a little weird. This is typically followed by an Alter Call.

These sorts of things were going on that night, and I decided to go up front, although I had never answered an Alter Call before. As I struggled to the center aisle, I decided I would NOT pray for my back. Obviously God did not need my help to know what I needed after 40 years; I would just pray for other people.

To this day I have no idea what or for whom I prayed, but after lying on the floor at the Altar for 20 or 30 minutes, Brother Stoneking came to me, reached his hand down, and said, "Brother Phelps, let me help you to your feet."

When his hand touched mine, I heard a loud thunderclap (but I do not think anyone else in the Temple heard the thunderclap), and the pain in my back stopped instantly!!! It has not returned in 20 years.

I told Jack Wagner, my Doctor at the time, and he said, "Let's have a CAT Scan, and find out what's going on."

When the Radiologist from Lansing came to Mount Pleasant to read the images, he said to Jack, "This is ***the worst mess I have ever seen***; this man should be paralyzed from the waist[106] down. Why is he still walking?"

Jack said, "I guess God had a different plan."

---

[106] The original has the charming variant phrase: "from the waste down."

The radiologist replied, "Everything I know says he should ***not be moving at all***, but you say he is a Scoutmaster, and he takes the boys canoeing, although he will not go backpacking with them? God must really have a different plan."

70. BRIAN

One day in 2010 or 2011 I received a phone call from Professor Jackson, Chairman of the Physics Department. "Can you meet me for breakfast?" and he gave a couple dates.

"Sure, I will meet you at Big Boy at 8 a.m. on Friday because I have Acoustics at 8 on Tuesday and Thursday."

Hum, I wonder what is going on. The Chairman has never invited me to come for breakfast before. When I arrived at Big Boy, Gail Moore jumped up and greeted me. Gail was the Advancement Person for the College or Science and Technology. Her first words were, "Do you remember Brian Taylor?"

Stutter. "Um, yes, but I probably have not seen him in 35 years!"

Then Brian jumped up and started to tell us a story, which I had actually lost from my RAM. This is my version of what I remember him saying, but what I write here may not be exactly what Brian said.

"You were fairly new on the faculty when I took freshman Physics. I got the worst grade in the class on the first hour exam. I wanted to drop the course and you would not let me. You said, "You are just finding it tough going and you get frustrated and do not know what to do. Instead of stewing about it, just come to my office and see me and I can get you straightened out fairly quickly."

He added that that semester he spent many hours in my office getting help. When I returned the second hour exam I announced that the class was improving and making good progress. The guy who had the worst grade on the first exam got the top grade on the second exam, and while it was still not good enough, the class was doing a fine job! Brian said he nearly jumped out of his seat, and his final grade was an A, only because I nursed him along!

So Brian's A was entirely my fault because I would not let him drop the class!

Eventually he graduated as a Physics major.

It was the fall of about 1977 when Professor McDermott, at that time Chairman of the Department, called me into his office and said, "We have a problem: We are short a Graduate Student. Who can teach three Lab sections for us? Can you recommend anyone?"

"Sure, Brian Taylor. I know he is looking for a job."

"Get on the phone and try to locate him and get him here as quickly as possible."

I suppose I phoned his Mother and got a phone number for him, but I don't really remember. When I reached Brian I asked, "Are you looking for a job?"

"Yes."

"Have you found a job?"

"No."

"Do you want a job? It does not pay very well."

"What would I have to do?"

"Start working on your Master's Degree and teach three Lab sections for us."

"When would I start, and how do I apply for the job?"

"You start tomorrow morning; Professor McDermott and the Dean have already approved and signed the appointment letter. The paper is on my desk waiting for your signature, and if you will sign it I will hand carry it to the Provost's Office and we will have you on the payroll before noon."

"Who is in charge of the Lab Assistants?"

"I am."

"OK, I accept, and I will see you in the morning."

Brian did not finish his MS in Physics with us, but has an MS in Petroleum Engineering and owns two Texas-based Oil Companies. When he asked what he could do for the Department, I said everyone has a different opinion, but we are saddling our Students with terrible Student loans, and, in my opinion, we need money for **endowed scholarship funds**, but you must decide what you want to do, and whatever it is, it will all help the Department.

Brian told me that his Daughter wanted to come to CMU and become a Physical Therapist but she had a tough first year at University, and on her own volition was retaking Physics, Chemistry, and every other PT prerequisite because, like so many freshmen, she had partied way too much and studied way too little. He was pretty proud of her turnaround and I had to tell him that, while I had no influence at all in PT, I would do whatever I could for her if she came up from Texas. I checked our admissions office several times. I think Penny eventually earned her DPT[107] somewhere else.

71. LAURA

Laura was a beautiful girl who sat in the first row in my Pre-Med class. I cannot look up the year because all my gradebooks have been recycled. One reason Laura stood out was her magnificent **BLACK HAIR, which just glistened.** As I was walking across campus one day she approached from the opposite direction and we stopped to exchange pleasantries. I complemented her on her hair and she said she was

---

[107] Doctor of Physical Therapy

growing it for "locks of love." She had a favorite Aunt who had no hair at all owing to Chemotherapy and they would make her hair into a wig for her Aunt.

"What a wonderful thing to do. She will be truly blessed, but I wish you did not have to cut it off; it is just beautiful."

"I thought you liked blonds."

"Well, Ginger is a blond, which is why I love blonds, but how can I not love your hair?"

Then Laura shocked me by telling me she was thinking about dropping out of the Pre-Med program. "I've been listening to you tell our class you must love your work, and if you don't, then change your major and do something else. I have always been interested in Dietetics; would you write a letter of recommendation for me to Harper-Grace Hospital in Detroit? They have the best Dietetics program in the State, and I might get a huge scholarship too, and I would have a leg up if I finish my Bachelor's Degree there."

"I will start it this afternoon, but you must get me the name and address of the person who should receive it."

"I'll bring you an envelope with a stamp later today!"

"No, don't do that. The letter must be on Department letterhead stationery: If it is just on plain paper you could write the letter yourself and forge my signature."

"Oh, I never thought of that. I know I can help hundreds more people by being a great Dietitian than by being a run-of-the-mill Doctor."

Later that afternoon she brought me the name and address of the recipient. Laura did transfer to Harper-Grace at the end of the fall semester, and I have often wondered about her adventures there, and what she has been doing since she graduated.

Now that I think about it, perhaps this just might be the first time I did my job right. Once in 42 years is better than 0 in 42 years. I might even earn a Paw Print for this!

72. Amy

Amy was in my Pre-Med class and needed to talk to someone about her life. She had been sitting on the porch with her Dad when he had a heart attack and she freaked out because she did not know what to do to save his life. Her Hero was her Aunt who was a Doctor, and Amy was determined to follow Auntie and become a Surgeon.

Her Aunt worked in some distant city and was often called to the Hospital in the middle of the night to treat a seriously injured individual. She frequently returned home only after 24 hours in the Hospital. Her Husband finally got tired of having no Wife and having a Baby-Sitter raising their children and eventually asked for a divorce. Auntie then hired Amy to come to her house for the summer to take care of the children while she was at work. Amy realized that being a full-time Surgeon had destroyed Auntie's family life.

When Amy met Hunter, who was also in the same Pre-Med class, she faced a terrible dilemma and came to talk to me. I supposed she knew I would listen and not pass judgment. Eventually I realized that Amy was saying she wanted to get married, raise a family, and have a life after the Doctor's office, but being on call 24 hours a day was not going to work, although her passion was still to be an MD and help people who needed medical attention. Fortunately, I had previously encountered a Physician's Assistant and learned about that profession, and thought Amy should consider it instead of Medical School. By being a PA, she could hang up her stethoscope at 5 p.m., go home, cook dinner, read bedtime stories to her children, spend time with her Husband, never be on call nights or weekends, and have the best of both worlds.

BULL'S-EYE! She immediately contacted her Aunt and had a long conversation. Auntie informed her that she was on the Board of Directors of a Medical School on the Cuyahoga River in Ohio that had a fine PA program. If Amy would apply there, she might be able to help her acquire scholarships and internships and other things that would ease the cost of her further education. In addition Auntie might even be able to influence admission decisions at any School to which she applied.

It was not long before Amy was admitted to that PA program. Shortly thereafter, Hunter decided he really wanted to be a Pharmaceutical Representative and spend his life visiting Doctor's offices teaching them about the latest wonder drug his firm had invented.

Mφm and I attended their wedding, and annually we receive a wonderful Christmas letter from Amy, who is now a Mother of two boys, is a PA Oncologist, and loves her work. Hunter loves his job as a Pharmaceutical Rep. They live in a nice suburb, the boys are thriving and life is GOOD. **Hallelujah, Jesus**!!! Two right in 42 years is better than 1 in 42 years. I might just catch on how to do my job right if I can just keep teaching.

73. ANN

I just cannot remember Ann's real name, so I shall call her Ann. Ann enrolled in my Pre-Med class sometime in the 1990's. She was a good Student, but not a great one, and came to my office for help a few times.

One day after we had gone over a particularly tough homework problem, she looked up at the clock, sighed, and said, "I have to go, or I will be late for my job."

"What do you do?"

"I am a Phlebotomist at the Hospital and I just hate it. I just hate going to the Hospital."

"If you hate going to the Hospital, why are you a Pre-Med Student?"

"My Father thinks the most important job in the world is to be a Pediatrician."

"What do you really want to do?"

"I want to be a Kindergarten Teacher!"

"Are you willing to spend your whole life getting out of bed and hating to go to work just to please your Dad?"

"No, I can't face that, but what can I do?"

"What does your Dad do?"

"He is a Refrigerator Technician for a grocery store," and Ann hung her head a little because of what he did for a living.

I had to say, "That is a very important job. I bet there are a thousand or more families that depend on him to keep all the frozen food frozen so it is safe to eat. Don't ever look down your nose at what your Dad does; perhaps he never had a chance to go to College. I suppose he has a million dollars of food to keep safe?"

"No, ten million, and, during the Holidays, twenty million."

"Wow, that is a very responsible position! Will you let me tell you my opinion of a Kindergarten Teacher?"

Sigh, "O.K."

"Of all the employees of any School system the Kindergarten Teacher is the most important person of all."

This was followed by a rather astonished, "**WHY?**"

"Because every kid goes to School eager to learn; they do not know anything about Mathematics or History or anything else, but they know they are going to learn a lot of things about a lot of stuff. If they have a good first year, you will set them up for life, because they will love School and love learning. They will thrive because you gave them a great start. Everybody must learn something new every day of his life or he might as well be dead."

"But what can I do?"

"What is your Dad's favorite treat, a banana split at Big Boy or a cup of Starbucks coffee? I cannot help you there, but it is absolutely critical that you figure it out correctly. Suppose it is a banana split. Thanksgiving is coming in a couple weeks; when you are home and there is a lull in the action, seize the moment and say, 'Dad, I must talk to you. Let's go get a banana split,' and when it comes **YOU PAY FOR IT!**"

"Why? I've never bought my Dad a treat before!"

"You have got to get his attention, and believe me, that will get his attention. Then tell him you just cannot face a lifetime of being a Pediatrician and going to the Hospital every day. When he asks what you really want to do, blame it all on me, and tell him Dr. Phelps' opinion of a Kindergarten Teacher, and see what happens."

Ann left for work with a little more bounce in her step than I remembered seeing previously.

A week or so after Thanksgiving, Ann came to my office and said, "Wow, paying for Dad's treat really got his attention, and guess what he said? 'Honey, if you want to be a Kindergarten Teacher, be the best one there ever was, and I can brag to my friends that **MY DAUGHTER IS A KINDERGARTEN TEACHER;** *THAT'S THE MOST IMPORTANT JOB IN THE SCHOOL SYSTEM.*'"

"Oh, by the way, I have already changed my major to Elementary Education and I won't be taking Physics 131 second semester. I have to go study now; I can't let Ginger down. I must do well on the final exam!!! I bet very few Kindergarten Teachers have a course in College Physics on their College transcripts and I want mine to stand out a little bit; I think it will help me get a great job!"

I have often wished that I could sneak into Ann's classroom and see her children thriving. I am sure she will not cancel Math for the day and disappoint her future Scientists. Good Heavens, did I do my job right a third time? At this rate I will have to grow more fingers and toes so I can count high enough!

74. Marie

With 120 Students in my Pre-Med class, a second class of 30 in Acoustics, and a third class of 32 in Physical Science for potential Grade School Teachers, it is clear that I did not have much time per week to help individual Students who needed it. The five office hours the Dean requires us to post just are inadequate, giving only 1.7 minutes per week per Student. Furthermore, no matter which office hours I post, it is likely that Students have classes in Organic Chemistry or Microbiology or other required subjects they cannot miss and so cannot come during posted hours.

My solution was to require all Students to form study groups of three to five Students, meet together as needed, and help each other solve the required homework problems and learn the lecture material. Only if they could not straighten each other out were they to come to my office any time between 7:30 a.m. in the morning and 5:00 p.m. I would not guarantee to help them because I might be helping another Student, or be in class, or a Department meeting, or otherwise be unavailable.

But if I was there, I would drop what I was doing, and meet them in the theory room where there were several large tables for them, and two whiteboards for me to write on. That way I could help all members of one study group at the same time, or accommodate two other study groups if they all had the same questions, which is actually quite common, because what stumps one Student often stumps another.

Marie realized that a good grade in Physics is absolutely essential for admission to any Medical program and in particular for her chosen profession, Physical Therapy. She formed a strong group and they diligently helped each other nearly every day. Her group would go to the theory room, and she would come to my office, put her head around the door jamb and say, "Dr. Phelps, we are stuck; can you help us?"

I was usually writing a weekly quiz or an exam question and I would invariably respond, "Just give me time to save what I am doing and I will be in Room 208 as soon as possible." Sometimes I made a pit stop on the way so they would not have to vzlp[108] for their lives!

Once in the theory room I would be greeted with five smiling faces, all eager to understand the material we were studying that week. None of them were Mathematicians and none of them were Physicists, but they gave their studies everything they could because they knew the final result would be worth all the toil and tears and effort expended. It was apparent that these were the top Students in the class.

Three or four weeks into the semester a Chinese Student, Tsong Ming, came to me. It was her first semester on campus, and she had just arrived from mainland China. She knew absolutely no one at all, but she needed to get into a study group, and asked if I could help her. The next morning I asked Marie to stay a few minutes after class and I told her I knew it violated my maximum of five Students in a study group, but would she consider letting Tsong Ming join her group?

Her group welcomed Tsong Ming with open arms and soon gave her the name "Magic." I had told Marie that I thought Tsong Ming would contribute more to her group than she took from it. After all, Chinese do not get an exit permit to study in the U.S. unless they are very good Students.

It was a real joy to have such a dedicated group of Students leading the class and I looked forward to their frequent "office hour" visits. How could anybody not love a Student who really wants to master the subject you are teaching? It is Students like this who make being a Professor a wonderful career.

---

[108] Fritz's Wife demanded that we take out this sentence, but we have chosen to encrypt a portion of it. Although reader discretion is advised, the key to decryption is explained in the footnote in the story "High School Chemistry."

International Students often wish they could see the inside of an American home, but they are seldom invited. I heard a story that Saddam Hussein hated the U.S. because not a single person invited him to their home for a meal while he was a Student at MIT.[109] How could I invite Tsong Ming to my house for dinner? It does not seem proper for a male Professor to invite a young Co-ed to his house under any circumstances. I asked my Wife if I could invite Tsong Ming and Marie to come.

"Yes, so long as you do all the work."

Tsong Ming was delighted with the invitation and Marie agreed so long as I did not do anything exotic. She thought a typical American evening meal would be best. I cannot remember what was on the menu, but we had a wonderful time and Marie took photographs of the event with her cell phone. Duh. In 2008 I did not know you could do that!

It was not long before we decided to buy our first cell phones. When I told my Pre-Med class that Marion and I had decided to get into the 20th century, not the 21st and that I had a unique ring tone, Marie immediately piped up, "I bet your phone barks instead of ringing."

"Do you want to try it and see if you are right?"

"Sure."

Every class needs a little comic relief once in a while. Marie dialed my phone number and the whole class erupted in hysterics! It must be that Marie had her antiquated Physics Professor figured out quite accurately.

A few months later Marie stopped to see me without her study group and asked me why I dropped everything and came running to the theory room whenever she stuck her head in my doorway? I could not answer! I had been doing it so long; I just could not think my way through

---

[109] Fact check: Saddam Hussein studied at the University of Baghdad.

to a suitable answer and I told her I would have to work on the answer and I would try to have an honest answer for her in a few weeks.

Eventually it hit me: When Professor Newbound told me I had passed my thesis exam unanimously, I told him, "I can never thank you adequately for what you have done for me." His answer was that he would be thanked 1000 times over if I would help my Students. I finally realized that I was just trying to keep my promise to Professor Newbound, the finest Professor I had ever known. By helping Marie, I was just trying to keep my promise, and that was extremely important.

After all, for a Scoutmaster to not keep his promise is terrible: How could I expect the boys in my Troop to keep their word if I did not keep mine? It is not important that the boys know, it is important that I just do it, because it is a major influence on how I live my own life. Thanks Marie, for making me realize how important it is for me to keep my word; I am so grateful!

During Marie's senior year she came to me and asked me to write a letter of recommendation for her and asked me where should she apply for Physical Therapy? She was interested in some University in Wisconsin, but I have forgotten which one. I told her I could not tell her anything specific, but I would give her some advice if she wanted to hear it.

"Sure."

I said, "You must investigate each program you are interested in and ask yourself several questions: Can you identify a particular aspect of Physical Therapy that interests you that is emphasized in one program and not another? Can you identify a particular Professor you want to study under?

"I cannot imagine what other questions are important to you, but you must decide **WHAT IS THE BEST PROGRAM FOR YOU**. You are the only person who can answer that question. I will write as many letters as you want; just tell me who I should send them to."

"Where do you want me to go?"

"I really want you to stay at Central. We have a fairly new program that is gaining a lot of respect, but I am prejudiced; don't listen to me and what I want. You must do what is best for you!"

I wrote letters to about five Universities and eventually she came to see me one more time. She said, "I have decided to accept the offer from Central; it will save me $50,000 in Student loans because I will get in-state tuition. That is one thing I had never considered!"

No question; that is one smart girl!

A year later she came to me and said, "I will be graduating from CMU on the first Sunday in May and my three year PT program starts on May 15th. Do you know anyone in the PT program that could help me? I just have to get off on the right foot and prove to my Professors the first day of class that I am a **Serious Student**!"

"I am sorry, Marie, I do not know a single Professor in that program, but I have an idea. Have you ever heard of Erica Wilson?"

"No."

"Erica is from the UP,[110] just like you, and was in my Physics class one year before you. She has just finished her first year of the PT program. I will write her an e-mail and ask her to contact you if she is willing to tell you a bit about your Professors and show you through the building."

Marie came to see me a few days later. "Guess what happened?"

"Tell me."

"All the girls in my cohort are assigned a mentor from the previous year's class and guess who my mentor is? Did you arrange that?"

"Marie, that has to be a "God thing." I am certainly not smart enough to assign Erica to be your mentor, and besides, I did not even

---

[110] UP – Michigan's "Upper Peninsula."

know they gave you a mentor." You are going to be best friends with that girl as long as you live.

"We are already best friends."

Nuts, I thought I was finished writing stories, but I guess I must write about Erica.

75. Erica, Part 1

Erica enrolled in my Pre-Med Physics class fall semester 2007. As the years have passed, I have become convinced that it was not an accident, but something that perhaps was **Preordained from the Foundation of the Universe**. I got to know Erica quickly after the start of classes. She was raised in Escanaba where her Dad was a Kindergarten Teacher, then High School Principal and finally Superintendent of Schools. Erica told me that when she was in High School and beginning to think about Colleges, she had absolutely no intention of ever becoming a "Troll" by attending a College or University "below the bridge."[111]

Then one day during her senior year her girl friend said, "Let's borrow a car and go to Troll Land and check out some Colleges during spring break." That sounded like a fun thing. They visited many Colleges in the Lower Peninsula that had a Physical Therapy program. Eventually her friend started driving towards Mount Pleasant, and Erica started saying, "This is a waste of time: I am not interested...."

Then, as they started into town, and long before they had seen even one building or a square meter of the campus, she announced, **"THIS IS WHERE I AM GOING TO GO TO COLLEGE!!!"** How can a dramatic about-face like this happen after years of saying, "I will not

---

[111] i.e., South of the Mackinaw Bridge in Michigan's Lower Peninsula.

become a Troll!!!" unless **God himself** plants it in your mind with super glue? There surely is no possibility of disobeying God if he gives you an order like the one he dumped on Erica!

Erica is a spunky, beautiful, fairly small blond and one of the first things she did was join the CMU Cross Country Team even though she had never participated in Cross Country in High School. But she was a Track Star and when she was a freshman in High School she was on her High School's varsity basketball team.

CM Life[112] often ran stories of Erica's exploits the year she was in my Physics class and I would cut out each article and give it to her before class so she would have a second copy if needed. This just reinforced my stereotype that small runners do better on long distance races than bigger runners, who seem to do better in short dashes and hurdles.

Why? Because every human body must remove lactic acid from the muscles as a person runs, and having a more compact volume would seem to help by reducing the length of tubing the blood supply must pass through. I have no idea whether this makes any sense to an MD, a physiologist, or an anatomist, or is just a stupid idea from someone who does not know anything about the human body and has not run a race in the 70 years since Grade School!

Erica told me her Hero was her big sister who was four years older than she was. Whenever she was facing a really tough class, she would think, "I'm scared I will do poorly, **but Krystal did it, and I can do it too." Then NOTHING could stop her from doing well.** My ideal class would be one hundred Students with Erica's weltanschauung![113]

Erica told me she came to Physics very early the first day of class because she had to stake a claim to the middle seat in the first row. After I

---

[112] The student newspaper.
[113] Weltanschauung: German for "world view, approach to life."

slowly looked at each Student's face without any change of expression, then looked at her and smiled, she knew Physics was going to be a good class and she would do well. Why? I cannot account for this, but pleeeeease let me know if you can!

76. Erica, Part 2

The CMU Physical Therapy program begins with one year of intensive study and then the Students spend time as apprentices in established PT clinics, obtaining experience applying what they learned on actual patients. They are closely supervised by a practicing Physical Therapist, often with many years of experience. Each "rotation" is three months long and the Students develop close relationships with their mentors who may very well answer questions from their Students long after the Students have moved on to other clinics. It is a wonderful program.

Erica's last rotation was at a sports clinic in Green Bay, Wisconsin. Erica's parents live in Escanaba, not that far from Green Bay. As graduation day approached, Erica thought she would apply at Bellin Health Hospital in Green Bay. They were searching for a staff Physical Therapist, and she asked me for a letter of reference.

I wrote Ms. Ortega who telephoned me and said she really did not want a written letter of recommendation but wanted to talk to me about Erica. I think we talked for at least two hours. I told Ms. Ortega I could not answer her questions: "Is Erica a leader? Is she this, or is she that?" I told her I always had 120 Students in my Pre-Med classes and my job was to help them learn enough Physics to do well on their M-CAT (or equivalent) exam. Besides, I had no method of measuring such things as leadership abilities, and I certainly was not smart enough to judge such things for myself. She would have to ask other references who might be able to help her with those questions, but I would tell her what I could about Erica.

I emphasized that she would be foolish to take what I said seriously because in I was so biased in Erica's favor I could not give an accurate evaluation. But I would do my best to tell her what I could because I thought it would reveal a lot about Erica's character, and if it was not important, Ms. Ortega should just ignore it and rely on her other references. Ms. Ortega was willing to listen, so I proceeded to tell her about what a wonderful Student Erica was because her Hero was her Sister whose example was so important when she was in High School and College. I told her how Erica helped Marie just because I asked her for help. I said that if she would hire Marie after she graduated, she would have the finest PT staff between Rochester, Minnesota and the Prime Meridian at Greenwich, England. I really dumped on the poor lady, laying it on several centimeters thick with a trowel.

Erica telephoned me later and told me Ms. Ortega offered her the job after checking only one reference. She apparently did not get many references from Physics Professors and took what I told her seriously. I often wonder whether Erica's supervisors have as high an opinion of Erica as I do. Admittedly, Erica can only walk on water if the ice is several centimeters thick, but is that the whole story? That is a fascinating question for which I have no answer.

Bellin Health put Erica on the payroll the day after her graduation ceremony at the beginning of May even though it would be unlikely that she would have her State License for Physical Therapy until June or even later. This gave her time to become well acquainted with Hospital procedures and to meet the Staff Surgeons, Nurses and other members of the PT team with whom she would work.

After about a year on the job, Erica told Fritz that she had a new friend that she was spending a lot of time with and it just happened to be a boy! Hummm, sounds interesting! Eventually Fritz received a refrigerator magnet that looked like a Green Bay Packer's football ticket that creatively said, **"SECTION 10, ROW 04, SEAT 14. SAVE THE DATE FOR THE WEDDING OF ERICA WILSON AND BRETT RODGERS, April 5th 2014."**

Fritz had an appointment with a Hand Surgeon and Occupational Therapist in Grand Rapids on the day before the wedding. Rick, who now lives in nearby Holland, Michigan, was willing to drive Fritz to Madison Wisconsin on Friday night and spend the night with Fritz's Grandson, Wu Hao, and his Wife, Becca, and then drive to Green Bay Saturday morning, attend the wedding at 1 p.m., stay for the reception at **LAMBEAU FIELD** and drive back to Holland on Sunday.

Rick and Fritz did all of that, but there was a slight change in plans as they started the return journey, heading South towards Milwaukee. Rick needed three or four hours to prepare for his Monday classes and if they could take the car ferry from Manitowoc to Ludington, it would replace eight hours of driving 700 km to Holland via Chicago, with a four hour boat ride and a 160 km drive from Ludington to Holland. The boys found a table in the aft cabin on the Badger[114] with an electrical outlet for Rick's Laptop Computer, and off they sailed across **LAKE MICHIGAN**.

The waves, as seen from the top deck, appeared to have a maximum height of 15 cm, making for a very smooth crossing. But the waves on Saturday, the day before, were said to have been well over one meter high, and crossings were very **ROUGH**. God was still watching out for fools and old folks, and the boys are not that old (except in dog years).

The wedding was lovely, but the best part for Fritz was spending time with his Son. Thank you Erica, Brett, and Rick for a wonderful weekend.

---

[114] The name of the ferry.

Part X. Ginger's Physics Exam

A little background probably would be good at this time and help the reader understand who Ginger is, and how she grew up to be a **Smart Physics Student.**

Ginger was 3/4 Cocker Spaniel and ¼ Dachshund but she looked like a Cocker that was 4 cm close to the road and 10 cm longer from the tip of her wet nose to the tip of her tail than her Mother, "Peaches." Because she was a BLOND, Dr. P knew she would be exceptionally **SMART** and started to teach her Physics from the age of 7 weeks.

77. Physics Problems #1 Zooming

Quite of her own accord Ginger started to **ZOOM** one day. She looked at us, grinned and then ran in a circle of about 6 meters diameter, just as fast as her 4 cm long puppy legs would take her. After making the first circle, she flopped on the grass and panted for about 25 seconds, jumped up and ran around the circle again. All the time we were yelling as loudly as possible, **"Zoom, Ginger! Zoom!!!"**

After that our favorite trick was to take her outside and yell, **"ZOOM, GINGER! ZOOM!"** and she would take off at a high speed, always stopping to pant after the first circle was run. A stop watch allowed us to obtain an average time for one rotation, from which we could calculate the angular velocity, ω, in radians/second (Prob. 1). This was a wonderful Physics exam question for the fall Pre-Med physics class. Dr. P. just needed to tweak it a bit by using random function generators so that each student had a *different diameter* and a *different time interval* for two rotations around the circle.

78. Physics Problems # 2-6

There is a wonderful comic strip of Mother Goose and Grimm in which little **TIMMY** has fallen down a well. **Lassie** (AKA Grimm) runs for help, but no one's at home. He looks for a ladder or rope but none can be found. Suddenly a freak earthquake causes a whirlpool to form in the well and little **TIMMY** starts to rotate faster and faster. Poor **Lassie** can only stand by helplessly and watch while she holds down the flush lever of the toilet.

What a great example of rotational motion! In the problems to follow, all numerical data are chosen by random function generators, so that each Student has a different numerical value for each quantity he must calculate. This makes it easy for the Professor to detect any cheating, as well as who is the cheater and who is the cheatee, which enables him to deduct points from the cheatee who was trying to help his dishonest friend.

Little **TIMMY** becomes **Atilla**, who is modeled as a point mass randomly chosen between 3.25 and 3.75 kg, the well is given a radius between 13 and 16 cm, and the time for two complete anticlockwise rotations around the well is set between 3.25 and 3.75 seconds. We now have enough information to calculate the answers to several interesting problems.

Prob. 2: Calculate Atilla's moment of inertia assuming Atilla is a point mass, and the axis of rotation is in the center of the well and is aligned along the $+Z$ axis of a Cartesian Coordinate system with the $+X$ axis East, and the $+Y$ axis North.

Prob. 3: Calculate Atilla's centripetal acceleration.

Prob. 4: Calculate the centripetal force on Atilla.

Prob. 5: Calculate Atilla's tangential velocity at the moment he is going West.

Prob. 6: Calculate Atilla's angular momentum. Remember that all tensors of Rank 1 must have directions associated with them (use unit vectors, i-hat, j-hat, and k-hat as needed).

79. Problem # 7 Doppler's Effect

Ginger had very acute hearing and perfect pitch. Ginger and Freddy the Physiker went to the Indianapolis 500 and had seats in the first row, about midway down the long stretch, so cars passed them going mostly in a straight line.

Part way through the race, Ginger began to notice that when cars made the far turn and approached them, she would hear a whine which was close to a note on the even-tempered scale. Then when the car passed them, the pitch would drop almost exactly one octave.

This was a very interesting observation, and she pawed through her saddle pack until she found her Freshman Physics Book and could look up the general equation for Doppler's Effect. Unfortunately it was not there, but Freddy the Physiker had derived it on the blackboard during class. No problem, Ginger just had to get out her class notes. After studying the equation for some time, she suddenly realized that she could use it to calculate the velocity of the racecars as they raced down the straight-a-way in front of them.

The computation was somewhat complicated, and doing all that Math in her head made her a little dizzy (but that is normal for blonds, isn't it?), so she licked Freddy on the Chin to ask him to check her solution.

Prob. 7: Assuming that the phase velocity of sound in air on race day was 343 m/s, according to Ginger, how fast are the cars going, as they pass our intrepid adventurers? Assume the cars are traveling in the $+X$ direction.

80. Problems # 8-12 de Broglie's Hypothesis

De Broglie is pronounced "de Broy," just in case your French is a little rusty. De Broglie's Hypothesis states that all material particles have an associated wavelength given by Planck's Constant divided by the linear momentum. This discovery makes for several very interesting problems in Quantum Physics that freshman Pre-Med majors can solve easily. The original wording of the problem was something like what follows.

Professor um ah, ah, Professor ah, um, er, Professor X (who will not otherwise be identified), became very concerned that his blond girlfriend would be diffracted as she passed through the people aperture (i.e., door) of their house. Assume ***significant diffraction*** occurs when the de Broglie wavelength is 10% of the width of the aperture, which in this case is 91.4 cm. Assume further that the nearest grass is 2.00 meters from the door, and that the mass of the Girl is 11.6 kg, the length of the Girl is 101 cm, and her entire length must be on the grass!

Probs. 8 & 9: Specify the Cartesian Coordinate System used, and calculate the maximum momentum and the maximum velocity the Girl can have if she is significantly diffracted as she exits the house.

Prob. 10: Calculate how long it will take the Girl to get onto the grass.

Prob. 11: Assuming the age of the Universe is correctly estimated to be 10^{15} seconds, calculate the ratio of the time interval calculated in Prob. 10 to the age of the universe.

Prob. 12: Should Professor X have a bucket and mop handy just in case the Girl does make it out in time?

When Freddy the Physiker was grading this problem, he noticed that one student commented, "Professor X definitely needs a mop and big bucket handy because Ginger surely does not have that big a bladder." Upon reading this answer, Freddy went back and read the problem twice very carefully, but could find no mention of Ginger in the problem. So Freddy asked the class why the student thought the Girl might be Ginger?

Jessica answered, "We have been using 11.6 kg for Ginger's mass all year, so we had a wild hunch and thought that might be a **CLUE** to the identity of the Girl. Then Jessica asked another question, "Why is Ginger always the smart one, and Freddy the Physiker always the stupid one in all our exam questions?"

That was an easy question for a change.

"It is because Ginger is a Blond!" whereupon all the blonds in the class leaped to their feet, threw a fist in the air, and yelled **YAAH!!!!!!**

A careful solution shows that the time for the Girl to reach the grass is about 10^{30} seconds which is about 10^{15} times the estimated age of the universe, and we can conclude that the wild hunch was indeed a fairly astute hunch, and the girl might indeed be Ginger. To Professor X the student's logic seemed impeccable.

81. PROBLEM #13 GINGER ON VECTOR ADDITION

When the ideas of vector addition (addition of tensors of Rank 1) were introduced, Ginger tried to think of a way to clearly show the absolute necessity of taking the directions of the individual Tensors into account. Her mind had been racing all night, and in the morning she decided to take a walk, which might help her get a better grip on the problem.

She established a Cartesian Coordinate system with the door of her dog house at the origin. She renamed the $+X$ axis as "East," the $+Y$ axis as "North," the $-X$ axis as "West," and the $-Y$ axis as "South." Then she left her dog house and walked 10.0 meters East, rotated 90 degrees anti-clockwise and proceeded straight ahead an additional 9.0 meters (North). Each segment of her path was 1.0 meters shorter than the previous segment and it was in a direction 90.0 degrees anti-clockwise from the previous segment. After each segment had been walked she plotted her path carefully on a sheet of graph paper using a scale factor of 1.0 cm ~ 1.0 meter.

Eventually she reached the end of the 1.0 meter segment and when she look around at her path and her graph she realized that the sum, S, could be found graphically by drawing a line from the origin to her final ending point. She then measured its length with a cm ruler and measured the angle S makes with the East axis with a protractor. To help Ginger keep track of the various path segments she labeled them sequentially: A_{10}, A_9, A_8, etc. (that is A_{10} represents the 10 meter segment, and A_1 represents the 1 meter segment). Then, in a moment of insight, she realized that if S represents the sum of the paths she could write:

$$S = A_{10} + A_9 + A_8 + A_7 + A_6 + A_5 + A_4 + A_3 + A_2 + A_1$$
$$= \sum_{i=1}^{10} A_i .$$

Prob. 13: Find the coordinates of the tip of A_1.

82. Problem #14 Gingerball

This is a proof that speed ≠ the magnitude of the velocity, in spite of many textbook authors who assert the contrary.

As we have seen already, Ginger is very good at zooming in circles. She decided one day to invent a new game which she named Gingerball. It is sort of like baseball, but is played on a circle and not on a square. She drew a large circle with a 5 m radius on the front lawn (a larger diameter circle would run into the fence around Freddy the Physiker's garden).

Ginger chose a convenient point on the circle to be **home plate** and marked it with a piece of cloth which she held in place with four landscaping nails. Then, using the compass, which was still set to draw a 5 m circle, she struck arcs starting at **home plate**, intersecting the circle. The right the point of intersection she marked 1st base and the left point of intersection she marked 5th base. She proceeded to strike additional arcs using 5th base as origin and located the position of 4th base and so on locating the position of 2nd base and 3rd base.

To slow the game down, Ginger chose to use a whiffle ball instead of a standard baseball, but all rules are now exactly the same as a little league baseball game. The pitcher pitches a whiffle ball, the batter whacks it, and runs to whatever base he can reach without being put out.

To illustrate the difference between a tensor of rank zero (**speed**) and a tensor of rank 1 (**velocity**) we have to calculate the average speed of the runner and also his average velocity for each base reached. Because **EVERY** Tensor of Rank 1 **MUST** have a direction specified (or the grade for that problem is zero), we can draw a tangent to the Gingerball circle at home plate, choose the right half of the tangent line as our $+X$ axis, and measure the directions to the various bases relative to $+X$ with a protractor. After doing this problem in class, Freddy the Physiker often has his students take meter sticks and a stopwatch and play Gingerball in the halls outside his lecture room, obtaining experimental data for a rectangular ball field.

In a regular baseball game, a batter who makes an extra-base hit[115] cannot run to first base and then make an instantaneous right-angle turn for the dash to second base; the centripetal force on him is too great, and he must run in an arc between 1st and 2nd, and if he hits a triple, he must make an arc between 2nd and 3rd, but he cannot make an arc between 3rd and home.[116] He must slow down enough to run straight down the base path from 3nd to home.

However, in Gingerball the base paths are all arcs of a circle, and so it is easy to keep running at top speed if you hit a double, triple, quad, quint, or home run. The Gingerball problem is solved easily by drawing the playing field to scale and setting up a table with the type of base hit, time to run to that base, the distance (from which the speed may be calculated), and the straight line distance from home to a given base (from which the magnitude of the velocity may be calculated), and the required direction may be found from the geometry or measured with a ruler and protractor relative to $+X$ (or East).

The speed on, for example, a quint, is much higher than the magnitude of the velocity vector from home to fifth base because the path taken to fifth base was not a straight line.

---

[115] "Multibase hit" in the original.
[116] The author seems to think that "you cannot run out of the base paths" means that, when rounding third, you need to hug much closer to the straight line than in going from first to third via second.

Final Word to the Reader

This collection of short stories was written because my oldest Son, who we call Dr. IV, asked me to write down the stories I have told for more than 75% of a Century. Are they better written or told orally?

As I conclude, I would like to leave you with some brief, albeit scattered, advice I have picked up in my 80-some years on the Planet.

Encourage the mathematical ability in your children by counting train cars. You do not have to wait for a child to be ten years old! Start when he[117] is one and just do things that are fun for **YOU**; they will be fun for him if you are excited about it.

After nearly 50 years of teaching Physics and occasionally Mathematics and Fortran Programming, I have found that Students seem to learn best by studying examples followed by generalizing. To write good computer code, I solve the Math problem, then write computer code, and finally make the stupid block diagram and flowchart the Computer faculty love. I told my Eagle Scout Dan, a world class Programmer, I just cannot start with a flow chart. His response was, "Everybody does it your way."

It is more interesting to have Oscar the Otter sliding down a mud bank than a block of wood sliding down a board. But it's the same physics. Mostly just encourage your own child to do what he **LOVES**. Do not waste his life as a Thoracic Surgeon if he hates going to the hospital. The higher salary or prestige is not worth it.

---

[117] Author's note: Using the male pronoun is correct English, and a lot less pedantic than "he or she," which is the politically correct way to clutter up any written document. In questions of grammar I follow Strunk, and, *if somebody is offended, I say "HALLELUJA!"*

The best way to teach First Aid to Cub Scouts is to have a First Aid Race between dens to see who can put an arm sling **CORRECTLY** on a Victim or a magazine cast on a **broken** leg. A squirt of ketchup[118] makes it more realistic.

---

[118] The original had "catchup"

Made in the USA
Middletown, DE
06 May 2021